God's Love for Lovie

An autobiographical sketch of the life of Pastor Lovie Nichols

Written by
Pastor Lovie Nichols

Edited by Robyn Williams

ISBN: 978-1-5136-2263-7

DEDICATION

This book is dedicated to the memory of my late husband of 59 years, Eugene Nichols, Sr. I love you and I thank God for the amazing man that you were. May your legacy live on in the lives of our children, grandchildren and great grandchildren and for generations to come. I miss you so very much.

Acknowledgments

I thank God for the courage, the wisdom and the fortitude I needed to draw upon to write this book. Without God, I am nothing. Lord, I owe you my life! I thank my friends and family for pushing me to write and journal.

To my amazing children, I appreciate all that you have done for your father and I. I could not have asked for better children. I was determined that you would never experience the kind of upbringing that I did. You all have added such value to my life, and words will never express my gratitude for each of you.

Denise, thank you for always pushing me to grow and for making me think outside of the box! You pushed me to continue my education by helping me study, and taking care of household chores. You have grown to be an outstanding woman of God and I love you.

Brenda, thank you for always thinking ahead and putting things in order for me. Your mild-mannered nature is so calming and serene. When I see you walk into a room, I become joyful because I know that everything will be well. You are amazing! Always remember that I appreciate you being there for me and for taking such good care of your Dad and I.

Carmella, I appreciate your love and care for me. Thank you for the support you have given me throughout the process of writing this book. Words will never express my gratitude to you for your care, concern, love and support. You've been through a lot, but it's all working for your good. Eyes have not seen, ears have not heard the things God has in store for you.

To my one and only son, Eugene (AKA, "Nicky"), I thank God for your wit (your humor's just like your Dad's), and your prayerful spirit. Whenever I see you, I am full of Godly pride and I immediately know happiness. I thank God for giving me such an amazing son. Nicky, you are a strong, intelligent, kind spirit and my life is better because of you.

I often ask, "Lord, what have I done to deserve such amazing children?" I may never know, but God knows how thankful I am for you all.

To my God-daughter and daughter-in-law, Dr. Darlene, thank you for taking the time to put my words to paper. I thank God that He chose you as a helpmate for my son, Nicky. I love you as if you were my own.

Special thanks to those who inspired me to write this book: Author Robyn Williams, Elder Ozie Owens and Evangelist Alma Lyons.

Last, but never least, thanks to my amazing pastor and friend: John F. Hannah and First Lady, Anna Hannah. It continues to be an honor to serve under your leadership.

To my New Life Covenant Church Southeast family: I love you all!

Foreword

Pastor John F. Hannah

Congratulations Pastor Lovie Nichols on your first book! WOW…I am so grateful to serve as your pastor and shepherd. Your wisdom is amazing, your anointing is undeniable and your pure heart is a Godsend. I thank God for gracing New Life with such a jewel as you. When the Lord placed the charge in my spirit to begin the ministry of New Life, I answered the call.

After a few years in the seat of Pastor, I realized that many were joining the ministry who had never experienced the presence of the Lord. My calling was clear; I was ordained by God to create an atmosphere where souls would experience God's glory in such an unusual way until their lives would be changed forever, they would fall in love with Jesus and accept Him as their Lord and savior. In order to execute God's vision, I prayed that God would send seasoned, mature and well-rounded saints to the ministry.

Pastor Nichols, when you walked through the doors of New Life and joined, I immediately thanked God for answering my prayer! I appreciate your anointing, and I am proud to call you a member. It is my prayer that your story will be shared with thousands across the world, and lives will be changed forever. I celebrate you for answering the call and writing this book. Congratulations once again!

Your Pastor, John F. Hannah,
Senior Pastor New Life Covenant Church SE

Robyn Williams

"Are you journaling, Mother Nichols?" was the question asked. "Here a little, there a little," was the answer given me. This conversational dance began over ten years ago. It's rhythm and pace increasing as the years went by. Until recently when I received a text, email and phone call that said, "Robyn, my book is almost finished!"

Just as the creation of Mother Nichols' book was a process, so too was her journey to become the deeply anointed woman of God who she is today. We have the privilege of knowing and engaging with Mother Nichols as she walks through the victory laps of her life. Because of the authority she walks in, and who she is in God, all of us can be forgiven for wondering if she popped out of the womb speaking in tongues!

But don't we all have a before-and-after portrait of our walk with God? As it relates to Mother Nichols, what about the woman behind the anointing? Surely, there was a process that she underwent to arrive at the apex where she is today.

In God's Love For Lovie, it's that very journey that Mother Nichols invites us to partake of as she opens the curtains of her life to display the wounds, hurts, betrayals and victories that God has brought her through.

• • • •

Many years ago, when I first arrived at New Life, there were two women I latched onto: Evangelist Allie Trimuel and Mother Lovie Nichols.

Evangelist (as Pastor Allie Trimuel was affectionately known) was an awesome, yet gentle, soft-spoken woman of God. But when she prayed, this tiny dynamo could move heaven and earth with her anointing.

Evangelist Trimuel would leave you speechless wondering how in the world so much power could emanate from someone seemingly so frail.

Well, if Evangelist brought the fire, then Mother Nichols brought the thunder. Together, these two powerhouses were peas in an anointed pod. Both caused demons and devils to flee.

Sadly, time was not on my side as I did not have the privilege of working with Evangelist Trimuel on her memoir. Nevertheless, I count God faithful because He saw fit to allow Mother Nichols to complete the assignment that is this book. God is faithful and this book is the fulfillment of a promise.

Delighted, surprised, moved to tears, empowered...these are a few emotions you'll be challenged with as you immerse yourself in *God's Love for Lovie*. You're invited to soak up all the wisdom from her life's lessons presented herein.

Her testimony is riveting, yet rich with transparency. And at the end, you'll be treated to a sampling of what fellow believers have to say about our very own Pastor and Mother Lovie Nichols—a great woman of God whom we all love so dearly.

Evangelist Allie Trimuel would often say, "Don't wait until I'm gone to celebrate my life. Give me my flowers now..."

Likewise, enjoy the journey presented in these pages. But don't forget: Let's embrace, love on, and celebrate Pastor and Mother Lovie Nichols as she walks among us. We love you, Mother Nichols, and we thank you for all your effectual fervent prayers.

Yours in service to Him,
Robyn Williams

Minister Tom Hurley

I have been blessed to have my mother of origin (Colette Hurley) in my life even to this very day. But, in addition, God sent surrogate mothers into my life. Pastor (Mother) Lovie Nichols is one of my spiritual mothers whom I firmly believe God sent to cross my path, to teach me the discipline of a Prayer Warrior.

The first time I heard her lead opening prayer at one of our New Life Covenant worship services, I was struck by her warlike approach to prayer. In her distinct, raspy voice, this woman of small stature was clear to proclaim that she "HATES THE DEVIL." She would continue to bind up and cast out every spirit unlike God. She has never minced her words as to the narrow path we must follow according to the Word of God. You are either saved and live accordingly, or you are condemned with an expected dark end.

I know pieces of Mother Nichols' struggles, and she knows pieces of mine, but I believe our common bond has been our style of prayer to fight those battles. It is this guttural anger, hatred and disdain for the devil, who has come to steal, kill and destroy, that we share. It is difficult to explain, but I find myself literally grabbing ahold of the gates of heaven and shaking them ferociously as I petition God's intervention, while envisioning Mother Nichols kicking down the gates of hell, exclaiming her "hate for the devil."

The daily prayer line that she has established further cemented the high level of respect and admiration that I have for this Mighty Prayer Warrior. She has set the stage and led the charge for hundreds of men and women to join a prayer call at 5:30 a.m., Monday through Friday, and intercede for God's people and the lost. She has faithfully led this call regardless of her own personal challenges, and convenience.

My love and respect for this Mighty Prayer Warrior runs deep, and words alone cannot do justice to the impact she continues to have on my life.

I am grateful that she is providing a glimpse of her love story with God. I will be firmly grasping the gates of heaven in anticipation of a life-changing, mind-transforming shaking as she proclaims her disdain for the enemy, and announces the victory that comes through Jesus!

Mother, thank you for your sacrifice and perseverance. You have radically changed my life, and the lives of so many others. I Love You!

Minister Hurley

Table of Contents

Introduction xv

Chapter One 1
    Who Is Lovie?
    ▪ I Am ▪ 1
    ▪ My Upbringing ▪ 3
    ▪ My Formative Years ▪ 6

Chapter Two 9
    My Journey – Natural
    ▪ I Met Him ▪ 9
    ▪ Road To Salvation ▪ 10
    ▪ My Teaching Career ▪ 11

Chapter Three 14
    My Journey – Spiritual
    ▪ The Doctors Said 'No' ▪ 14
    ▪ God Saved The House ▪ 15

Chapter Four 18
    Church Hits
    ▪ Working In The Church ▪ 18
    ▪ Church Hurt ▪ 22
    ▪ The Recovery Process ▪ 27

Chapter Five 31
    Conclusion
    ▪ Rewards On Earth ▪ 31
    ▪ It All Works For Good ▪ 33
    ▪ The Miracles I've Witnessed ▪ 34
    ▪ God's Love For Lovie ▪ 41

• Stay The Course • 42
• My Prayer • 42

Chapter Six 43
In Their Own Words 43
• Who Pastor Nichols Is To Me • 43

Introduction

I never really reflected upon my childhood and upbringing until I reached my latter years. I wondered why my father was so cruel and abusive, and why my mother stayed with him. These questions plagued me as an adult and I would often pray and thank God for bringing me through such a horrible childhood, one that was rife with violence and abuse. As I reflected on the journey God had brought me through, the Lord revealed to me that it was time to take all of my thoughts, experiences, questions, answers and concerns, put pen to paper and write a book.

It is my heartfelt prayer that the Lord will bless you as you turn these pages to reflect, learn and grow from my life's story. I believe that this book will help many to understand that no matter what you go through in life, it all works together for your good as long as you love the Lord.

• • • •

CHAPTER ONE

WHO IS LOVIE?

▪ I AM ▪

My name is Lovie Mae Nichols, and I was born in Blytheville, Arkansas on July 5, 1937. My father was a Baptist preacher who attended church faithfully. He lived one way at the church, and another at our home. My mom and dad were not the most successful people in terms of relationships. In fact, my mother had two marriages prior to my dad, and he, himself, had six. My mother bore 15 children and lost eight of those during childbirth. My six siblings and I worked together to make sure that Momma had the things she needed to sustain us. Dad worked as a sharecropper, but his work was never really consistent. Growing up deep in the "country," my younger sister had the responsibility of bringing the cows in from pasture, while my responsibility was to milk the cows in preparation for lunch and dinner. Those were our daily chores, and we had no choice in the matter.

I remember one time I forgot to milk the cows because Sister didn't bring them in from the pasture. When my father came home and realized that the cows had not been milked, he grabbed a tree limb from the back yard. As I sat down for breakfast, he came into the kitchen and struck me with what seemed like all of the force he had. I nearly blacked out! It was then that I realized the ugly truth that my father was an abuser, and a bully.

Although this was one of few times his abuse was directed toward me, by this time, sadly I was used to witnessing his abusiveness to others: Namely my mother and all of my siblings. My father's words were damning and his threats were relentless. On one occasion, my father was in bed and mom was singing melodiously an old song entitled, "You're Gone to Need the Love of Jesus, Yes, Indeed." I loved her singing, but apparently, that day, dad didn't. He woke up and shouted, "Shut up!" He then ran into the kitchen and before I knew it, he'd punched mom dead in her mouth. I was horrified and so afraid, I jumped up and hid behind the stove.

There was another occasion when Momma was sitting on a stool knitting a quilt, minding her own business. Dad came into the room and knocked her flat off of that stool. No rhyme, no reason—just because. But this time, seeing my mom lying nearly lifeless on the floor, my brothers were so angry they began to hit him. Dad became infuriated! He grabbed a large, iron rod from the side of the fireplace and hit both of my brothers in their heads. Blood was everywhere, and there was complete mayhem in the house! After this day, my dad was on the warpath, beating every person in the household, including my mom. My mother would never stand up for herself; she would never talk back and in all of the years I knew her, she never spoke badly about my father. This confused me to no end, but I was a child, so my opinion meant nothing.

Once our chores were completed, Sister and I would walk to school together. The school was a small building with one room, and there were not many children at school whom I called friends. As a small child, I carried my wounds within me and I had no real desire to have friends. In those days, I was a loner and that was good enough for me.

▪ MY UPBRINGING ▪

Growing up in our household, it was all work and no play. Happiness only came whenever my father was away. My siblings and I would be happy to see him go, and sad to see him return. The moment Dad's truck pulled up to the house, all play ceased and we would all scurry to find some work that our little hands could do. A sense of fear would infuse the house because we never knew what mood Dad would be in.

When I reached the age of 14, after many years of horrid, violent abuse, my parents separated. My sister and I were forced to stay with our father, while my siblings who were adults struck out on their own. I still remember the day that my mother left us. It was a Sunday morning in 1952, while my father was at church preaching. Realizing the tortuous toll that all of the beatings were having on my mom's health, my brothers talked to Mom from sunup until sundown, trying to convince her to leave the house. At approximately 6:00 p.m., my mom succumbed to their persuasions. She packed her bags, left a small note and walked out of the house. I remember being very happy that she'd made up her mind to finally leave.

Sister and I were dropped off at a neighbors' home, "Mrs. Richardson." I'm unsure of what happened when Dad got home, but he did come and pick us up from Mrs. Richardson's house.

Once Mom left, things were different. Dad was much nicer and his abusiveness quieted down a bit. With Mom removed from the home, Dad was not a changed man, but a very different man. He would take us to the drive-in movie theater, and I could go to baseball games now. He tried to do things to make us happy. He cared for my sister and I and assisted us as best he could. Once I graduated from the 8th grade, Dad took me to the O'Bannon High School where I began my journey into young adulthood. In high school, I played basketball and was a pretty good student. I even made a few friends and joined a few clubs. I remember in my senior year, joining a singing competition. I joined the competition just to see if I could win. I never really had the desire to sing, but I did want to see if I could win. Lo' and behold, I entered, sang and won! I am still tickled pink to this day that I won a singing competition.

In 1955, at the age of 18, I was preparing for my high school graduation and decided to visit my mom in Niles, Michigan. While there, we spent quality time together which I thoroughly enjoyed. I received a letter from my dad asking me to come home as he was gravely ill. My Mom decided to come back to be with me because she wanted to see me graduate. I asked her if she was sure that she wanted to go back to where Dad was. She said, "Yes, because I want to see you graduate."

Mom bought me a beautiful dress to wear to the graduation. I was so excited! My brother in-law tried to convince Mom not to go back to Dad's house. He said, "Mom, if you go back there, you will be dead in less than six months."

She gently smiled and said, "Son, I will be fine." We went back home to care for Dad only to discover that he was not sick at all. Instead, he was simply up to his old tricks. For me, however, this was a bittersweet time because I had my mom back, but I also feared that my brother inlaw's words would come true.

In May of 1956, two weeks before my graduation, my Mom was lying in the bed. Dad asked her to fix his breakfast and she replied, "I'm too sick, Mr. Willie." Dad's response was, "You're not sick. Get up and fix my breakfast!" In an effort to calm Dad down, I offered to fix his breakfast, but Dad yelled, "No, I want her to fix it!"

Mom struggled out of bed with the little strength she had left and went into the bathroom to wash her face before preparing his breakfast. After washing her face, she said these words: "Mr. Willie, you are going to worry me to death." Mom walked into the kitchen and suffered a massive stroke. My mom was put back into the bed by my dad. He had such a sad and fearful look on his face. He went and got the doctor. The doctor came and gave my mom a shot. He said that if she made it through to Monday morning, she could be admitted to the hospital. But he knew that she was not going to make it. Mom had another massive stroke on Saturday morning. By Sunday night, I, too, knew my mother was not going to make it. So, I got into the car and was going to the pay phone to call my brothers and sisters (in those days, we didn't have mobile phones. We didn't even have a landline telephone in our home).

I got almost to the pay phone when the cars' engine light began to blink! Suddenly, I felt a pull in my spirit. I said, "Awww, God, no!" I turned the car around and drove back home. I opened the door and my mother was taking her last breath. I called out to my mom when Mrs. Richardson, said, "Let her go, baby."

I didn't say anything else, and Mom closed her eyes and made her transition. My mom had talked about death all week before she died. She said that she did not want to suffer, and she didn't. My mother passed away on May 7, 1956. Her funeral was on May 14, 1956, Mother's Day. The dress she purchased for my graduation was the dress I wore to her funeral.

My heart was broken, and my life felt like it was shattered. But even though I was heartbroken and sad, I also knew glimmers of happiness because my mom would not have to suffer from my dad's abuse any more. A few days after we laid my mother to rest, we went home one night and strangely, all the lights in the house were on. My dad was sitting in a chair with his head back as far as it would go. When my sister and I walked in, he raised his head up and said, "Oh my! I am so glad you're here. Something had hold of my head and would not turn it loose." My sister and I looked at each other and laughed. We said, "Momma."

▪ MY FORMATIVE YEARS ▪

After Mom died, I found myself angry with my father because I believed that she died as a direct result of his abuse. I continued to re-live her words prior to her stroke, "Mr. Willie, you're going to worry me to death." Those words would haunt me, replaying over and over in my head. I knew that the only one who could help me move on, was God.

I'd always wanted to have a relationship with God, but I just didn't know how. As a little girl, I would often pray to God and ask Him to help me, lead me and guide me, but I never really knew if He was listening. I remember how, as a little girl, I would walk outside and stand by the side of the house talking to God. I'd ask Him, "God, am I Your child? Do I belong to You, and if so, why is my family like this?" I would ask God to let me have a good husband, not someone like my daddy. I would ask God to help my father to control his temper.

The truth was, I loved my father because he was really good to me. But at the same time, I hated him because he was always so abusive to my mother. How could I survive with these two strong emotions dwelling inside of me? It was such a struggle. Although I never heard an audible answer from God, when I talked to Him, I would always feel a calm peace in my spirit. I still longed to know God. And furthermore, I even longed to forgive my father.

I would often talk to my eldest brother about my feelings. It was my brother who served as the conduit to building my hope and trust in God. My brother, who was much older than I, would ask me such sincere questions about my feelings and he would always give me life-changing answers. My brother assured me that God was in control of my life.

I remember one day pouring out my heart to my brother and explaining that I did not understand how my mother could stay with a man who was so abusive. I asked him how they even met and married in the first place. My brother explained that our parents had met because of a family member. And, after knowing my father for only one week, Mom became pregnant with me. Once her pregnancy became known, they got married. I wasn't shocked, but I did understand a little better. They didn't marry for love; it was because of me. Once I realized this, the hatred I had in my heart for my father went away and never returned.

My hatred was no longer warranted. Being upset and disappointed was understandable, but hate did not belong in my heart. I now know that removing the hatred was orchestrated by God. I was able to move on and live my life with more clarity. All the bad things from my childhood worked together to make me who I am. If it had not been for my father's actions, I would not be the person that I am today.

On his good days, my dad taught me how to be a young lady, how to respect myself, and because of him we had to go to church. For this, I will forever be grateful. I remember one Sunday as I was playing the piano, he asked me to come out to the car. He said, "Lovie, I am so surprised at you. I never thought you would do this." I had left some cigarettes in the car's glove compartment. I felt so bad and ashamed that my dad saw those cigarettes. The following week, I planned to leave home. I wanted to go to college but my dad did not have the money to send me, so I was going to live with my brother.

• • • •

CHAPTER TWO

MY JOURNEY – NATURAL

▪ I MET HIM ▪

After graduating high school, my elder brother found the finances to send me to college in New York. Prior to leaving, I stopped in Chicago to visit my brother and his family. While staying with him, there was a group of young men who sang in a quartet, and they would often rehearse in the apartment where my brother lived. One man in particular (Eugene) noticed me and asked my friend if he could meet me. It was a hot day in June of 1956. My friend brought this tall, handsome man over to the house and introduced him to me. I immediately looked at him and thought, "Well, he's nice looking. Very pleasing to the eye."

Eugene would come over after his rehearsal every Saturday and spend time with my family—even though his true intention was to spend time with me. I really enjoyed his company, and I especially enjoyed his sense of humor. Not only did he make me laugh, he was handsome and extremely nice. We went out on a few occasions and enjoyed spending time together. In September of 1956, Eugene Nichols asked for my hand in marriage. I was so excited and of course, I said yes!

The next month, Eugene's mother died. I attended her funeral in Mississippi with him. I got a chance to meet his family, and what a beautiful family he had. On our way back home, we stopped in Missouri at my dad's home and Eugene asked my dad if he could marry me. My dad talked with him, and his answer was yes. In January of 1957, Eugene and I became husband and wife.

We began our family and had four beautiful children; three girls and one boy. I absolutely loved being a mother and wife. After each one of my children was born, I would go back to work. We did not want anyone else keeping our children. Eugene worked nights, from 4:00 p.m. to 12:00 a.m., so he kept the children during the days while I worked. He was the one who took them to their doctor's appointments, and he would also see them off to school or drive them. Eugene was the best husband and father!

▪ ROAD TO SALVATION ▪

My husband, my two brothers and I had a little club. We would have "quarter parties" in our home where everyone was charged a quarter for admission. One night, we rented a place and had our party. Half way through the party, I did not feel right. I promised myself that I was not going to another party as long as I lived. I did not know then what God was doing. I have not been to another club party since that day.

Praying was something that I found I loved to do. There was a lady in our building who would always have prayer meetings in her home. I would sit on the steps and listen to her pray. I was not able to attend her prayer meetings because my children were too small and I couldn't leave them. I loved to hear her pray and it made me want to know God for myself. One day, I got up the nerve to make my way over and chat with her. I told her how I loved to hear her pray, and that I wanted to know God for myself. She began to talk with me about what it means to be saved, and to know God personally. I absolutely loved our conversation and my heart was softened. She invited me to church, so I found a sitter and I went that same night.

During the service, I could feel the presence of the Lord and when the pastor made the altar call, I gave my heart to God, which was in December of 1965. His presence was so strong until I began to speak in tongues, cry and thank God for saving me. And from that time on, I have never had a mind to go back into the world and do any of the things I had done before. I was a new creature in Christ Jesus. I went home and told my husband that I was "saved." He did not fully understand, and was somewhat confused. He called his grandmother and she told him that he would understand as time goes by. At this point, I was saved, but my husband was not. However, I believed that God would save him eventually.

▪ MY TEACHING CAREER ▪

In 1968, I was looking for work and someone told me about a job at Hess Upper Grade Center. I went over to talk with the principal. I asked him if he was hiring. He said, "Yes, do you want to work here?" I told him yes and he instructed me to take a letter he gave me to the Board of Education. The Board hired me that very day. When I started at Hess Upper Grade Center, the principal had left on another assignment. No one at the school gave me an assignment, so I resigned myself to keeping the children out of the hallways and assisting the teachers in their classrooms. But, most of the time I was a substitute teacher until I got my own homeroom in 1988.

I accepted a job as a teacher's aide and would serve as a substitute teacher when needed. I discovered a passion for teaching and the assistant principal urged me to complete my education and obtain a degree so that I could teach full-time as opposed to working as a substitute. There was a program which allowed personnel to obtain a degree for free. At the advice of my assistant principal, I submitted my application and was accepted. Although, I didn't go to New York for college, I was able to complete my education free of charge. I know the favor of God was on my life because he allowed me to cross paths with another student who was a few years ahead of me. This student would share her notes with me; which were absolutely meticulous! I read her notes and studied them. I was able to pass every class with flying colors because God allowed her help to pave the way.

During my educational journey, my husband was so supportive. He continued to work nights and would watch our two children during the day while I worked. I graduated college and applied for a full-time job as a teacher. There was an entrance exam that I was nervous about because I was not a good test-taker at all. I asked God to have mercy on me and somehow waive the entrance exam. To my amazement, right before I was scheduled to take the entrance exam, they suspended the requirement and I was not required to take the exam. Four months after I was certified, the suspension was lifted and all new teachers were required to take the test. Only God would do that for me! I was assigned to the Charles Evan Hughes Elementary School as a full-time teacher!

During my years of teaching, God told me to pray in my classroom, so I would pray each morning. Next, He said, "Pray for the children." I began to pray for the children each morning, and did so again at dismissal time. I also began to pray for my children during their 8th grade graduation. I decided to write to the President of the United States to see what he had to say about praying in school. The president's response was, "There isn't anything wrong with praying in school if you are not disturbing anyone." I had collected 6,000 signatures advocating prayer in the school...so thanks to God I got prayer in my school. At the beginning and ending of each school year, I would lead my principal and teachers in prayer.

I absolutely loved being a teacher and imparting knowledge and wisdom to my students. I remember once when my job was challenged because I needed 34 registered children, and I only had 33. In those days, in order to constitute a full classroom, each teacher needed a minimum of 34 children. I prayed and asked God to intervene because I needed one more child. I called my good friend, Lorraine Allen, and asked her to pray as well. She paused for a while and then said, "Lovie, I see three children coming into your room." I said, "Lorraine, all I need is one more, not three!" She laughed and said, "Well, Lovie, I see three." We laughed and ended the call. The next day, three additional children walked into my room and I was amazed! From that day until the day I retired, I never had any further issues with low attendance.

• • • •

CHAPTER THREE

MY JOURNEY – SPIRITUAL
▪ THE DOCTORS SAID 'NO' ▪

In January of 1965, my friend invited me to church with her, to St. James Church of God In Christ. I walked into the church and the Lord said to me, "This is where I want you to be."

I joined St. James Church of God In Christ under the pastorship of Bishop Jesse Campbell. He was an anointed Prayer Warrior who would always say, "God can do anything but fail." I always believed anything God said through His word, and I was so strong in faith. I would listen to Bishop Campbell preaching and teaching and I was excited about my own spiritual journey. I had two beautiful daughters, but longed for a son. Unfortunately, my body did not align with my desire. The doctors diagnosed me as barren because my fallopian tubes were blocked, and my cycle was irregular. Several medical professionals informed me that I would never have another child because of the issues with my body. Still, I longed to have a son, so I went to Bishop Campbell and asked him to pray.

Bishop Campbell prayed for me to have a son. I just believed in my heart that God was going to grant my request, even though the doctors said I would never bear another child. After Bishop Campbell prayed for me, my husband and I conceived a few months later. The doctors were amazed! When the time of delivery came, our son was a breach and could not be delivered. The doctors really didn't know what to do, so they agreed to let me just rest in hope that the baby would turn. I was in such pain, but the saints were praying. After several hours, our son,

Eugene ("Nicky") Nichols, Jr. was born…all seven pounds and eight ounces of him! I remember that once he was birthed, he didn't cry right away and the devil whispered in my ear, "I'm going to kill him." I said, "No you aren't, devil. God would not give me a miracle son and take him away." I rebuked the devil immediately and spoke God's word. Needless to say, Nicky is now a powerful man of God, married with children, happy and healthy!

After my son was born, my body reverted back to its barren state. Sometime later, I joined the Old Landmark Church of God Holiness in Christ under the pastorship of Bishop R.L. Mitchell. I remember once while in church, Bishop Mitchell began to prophesy and said that someone in the sanctuary that day had a condition in their body, but God was going to heal them right now. I went to the altar for prayer, and Bishop Mitchell prayed for me. I remember feeling a cut in my stomach and a heavy hand inside. The pain was great. I walked back to my seat thinking, "Wow, I feel more pain now than I did before the prayer."

The next day, my cycle came and I was so afraid! I called the doctor but could not get an answer. My husband reminded me that I'd been in
the prayer line the night before. I now know that the
pain I felt was the pain of God's supernatural healing.
After the prayer, my husband and I conceived a baby girl
and her name is Carmella Yvette Nichols! My body was
regular from that day forward, and I was never again
diagnosed as barren.

▪ GOD SAVED THE HOUSE ▪

I was living a saved life, but my heart was heavy because neither of my children, nor my husband were saved. I was the only one saved in my household. One

Sunday while seated in church, I looked back to where my children were sitting, and the presence of God came upon me so strongly, I said, "God save my children!" The following Monday, my son came into my room and said, "Momma, I'm saved!"

I asked him, "When did you get saved?" He replied, "Momma, I got saved last night, in my room." I was really excited about his confession. He asked to go to church the next night, and was baptized with the Holy Ghost with the evidence of speaking in tongues. Nicky was serious about his relationship with God, and wanted to go to church all of the time. Rain, shine, sleet or snow he would say, "Momma, let's go to church! I'll pray, and you drive!" He was determined to serve God.

At the age of seven, Nicky praised God so much that one day he was outdoors praying for the children in the neighborhood. A neighbor was so excited that she came to my door and said, "Mrs. Nichols, your son is pushing the kids to the ground and they are falling out."

My husband and I went outside and lo' and behold, Nicky was having a church service and the children were experiencing the presence of God. That was something to see! Shortly thereafter, Denise, Brenda and Carmella similarly confessed a hope in Christ and were saved. My husband did not attend church, but would look on as the children and I went. I would always pray and talk to my husband about being saved. The Lord said to me, "Don't say anything else to him." I obeyed.

One day I was in the kitchen and noticed that my husband had fallen to the floor. I asked him what had happened. He said, "I don't know. I just fell in the floor." He was baffled and confused by what happened. The following day, I explained that the experience he had was God dealing with him. That next day, which was Sunday, my husband came to church and walked down the aisle to give his life to Jesus. God delivered him that very Sunday from everything he was doing. He never returned to his old ways.

Thank you, Jesus! My entire household was saved!

• • • •

CHAPTER FOUR

CHURCH HITS
▪ WORKING IN THE CHURCH ▪

I absolutely loved working in the church! I served on the usher board, I was a Sunday school teacher, I worked as the YPWW (Young People Willing Workers) teacher, I sang in the choir, served as a part of the pastor's aid committee and cleaned the pastor's office. I even picked up several of my students on occasion and brought them to church with me. Because I worked at the local school, I was able to witness to the young people who were in the street gangs and invite them to church. It wasn't long before I was renting a bus and shuttling all of my children who wanted to go, to church. Many young people were saved and filled with the Holy Ghost during this time.

God blessed me to have a close relationship with my pastor and everywhere I served, the pastor would know precisely where I was. If things were out of order, I'd tell the pastor and then I'd go into prayer. I was also a dreamer, and would often tell Bishop about my dreams. When the Lord would allow me to dream, I could see when people were not living Holy and Bishop trusted me to advise him of what I'd seen. I shared many things with him about the people of God. Bishop Campbell was extremely open in permitting me to share my dreams, and this, to me was such an honor.

In 1969, Bishop Campbell was diagnosed with a terminal illness. I was blessed to serve as his personal aide for an entire year. I remember as the shades were closing on Bishop's life, he turned to me and asked me one question: "Lovie, what is God saying?" I said, "Bishop you will be at church the first Sunday in September." He said, "Say what you mean." I said again, "Bishop you will be at church on the first Sunday in September." He replied, "Ok, I will meet you then." Just as the Lord had told me, Bishop Campbell was at church on that first Sunday in September…laying in a casket. It was his funeral service. I didn't know that God had prepared me for Bishop's death. When he died, I began having severe headaches. The lord reminded me, "You know how I walked you through this situation." There is nothing that God can't take you through, and I am so grateful.

After Bishop's passing, the Lord directed me to join the Old Landmark Church of God Holiness in Christ under the pastorship of Bishop R.L. Mitchell. I did not want to go, because I had other plans. I remember when God directed me there, I was surprised because I did not have a ride to this church, and it was quite a distance away. The Lord provided transportation for me, and ultimately I was able to drive there on my own. I worked at Old Landmark, just as I had when I was a member of St. James. It was during this time that the Lord opened the door for me to serve as a deaconess, where I would help take up tithes and offerings twice per month. His offerings increased, and I was honored to serve in this capacity.

I had become a Prayer Warrior and would pray, fast and seek the Lord regularly. Fasting for several days at a time was not uncommon for me because I loved God so very much. I wanted the people to know God in a real way, and to that end, I would follow the voice of the Lord and pray for people as He led. I was humbled that God thought enough of me to use me to bless His people. There were times when God would tell me to seek Him, and I would but then I'd stop. That was not what God wanted. He wanted me to be consistent.

This was the year of our convocation. I said to myself, "I am not going to work this summer. I am going to seek the Lord." I told myself that my mother prayed three times a day, and Daniel prayed three times a day so that is how I am going to pray and fast when the Lord leads me to. In July, the convocation began. I was getting ready for church one morning and I asked God to do something in OLMC that night, that had never been done before in that church. I was not asking Him to do it through me. I just wanted the people of God, to see the movement of God.

The praise service that evening was powerful. The Lord said to me, "Go pray for that sister." I stood for a while, and then He spoke again. I went over to the sister he was referring to and said, "God told me to pray for you." She raised her hands and I prayed. As I was going back to my seat, the spirit of God turned me around. He didn't say anything, it was like I was led by a string. I went to ten people, hugged each of them and they all fell under the power of God.

The entire church was standing and staring in awe! This was something that had never happened at OLMC. My Bishop was standing, looking on. He said, "Let the lord use you, Sis. Nichols." After that night, the Lord would use me in the same way. My eyes would fall upon a person, and I would feel the pull to go pray for them during the praise service or worship service. I prayed for many of the saints and God healed, delivered and set them free.

Although I felt the call to the ministry in 1971, it wasn't until 1992 that I was actually sent. After the night of the convocation, God told me to pray for the minds of the people, pray for the brothers, pray for healing and Bishop gave me permission to pray for those groups. God really moved in those areas. Finally, God said to me, "Have a healing service every third Sunday night." Bishop also gave me permission for that to happen.

If you obey God and keep His commandments, He will take you and use you in ways which you can hardly believe. God would remind me often, "I CALLED YOU AND I CHOSE YOU TO HELP DELIVER MY PEOPLE."

Sometime later, I began to feel that my time was over at OLMC, but God said to me, "No, if you go now you will not complete the work I sent you there to do." So, I stayed until September of 1993. My last assignment was to visit 12 churches and preach, "Guard Your Heart." These churches were all under Bishop's leadership. God moved in these twelve churches in such a powerful way, that no one had any doubt that it was God.

I am so humbled because the Lord used me at Old Landmark to pray for His people, and the Bishop was extremely open to the calling of the Lord on my life. Praying in this capacity was the defining of the ministry that God entrusted within me. I continued to work at Old Landmark until God led me to work with another local church under the pastorship of a young man and his mother. This experience would change my life forever.

Before I ventured to the next church (I had no idea I was going to the church I went to), God directed me to stop at this place and help them with a meeting that He was going to set up. On a Monday evening, August 2, 1993, as I was leaving my bedroom, He said to me, "Call the First Lady, Sis. Adam, in Niles, Michigan and talk to the pastor of the church." I felt like I was dreaming. I phoned her, and when God told me to pray with Sis. Adam, I did. After we finished talking and praying, Sis. Adam said, "I am going to call the pastor now."

She would have a one-week meeting each month. She called it the "Week of Consecration." Sister Adam called and "Pastor Cruz" (not her real name) was there the next day. The meeting began. The church was in a very small town with a population of about 200. The meeting lasted five weeks straight. Around 100 people came up to be saved. During the weeks of service, members of my own family were saved; five nieces, one sister and three nephews were delivered, and saved. Some who were shacking-up got saved, and then married; some were filled with the Holy Ghost. One of my nephews who attended is now a pastor.

God changed that little village. Before the meeting, they would meet up at each other's houses, use drugs, play cards and get drunk. God answered my prayers. I wanted my family to really hear the true Word of God. God said in His Word, "I will perfect those things that concern you." God is true to His Word. Over the next two weeks, people came from other places. After the meeting was over, God lead Pastor Cruz to open up a church in another area of that city, which was a blessing. Because I obeyed God and followed His leading, lives were changed. I am so grateful to have obeyed Him.

I pray that everyone who reads this chapter will let God save, deliver and use you for His glory!!

▪ CHURCH HURT ▪

As God led me to the next church, the first pastor in that church was a young man. During the times that he was in charge, the services were powerful. He was pastor for about 10 years. While with this ministry, I saw God work in a way that I'd never seen Him work before. I witnessed miracles, signs and wonders. I was comfortable at this church because I knew the pastor and we had worshipped together at St. James. We worked together, witnessed to people in the neighborhoods and held overnight services. Lives were changed like never before. It was something to see!

I remember once having an outside service and people walking the streets would stop and enjoy the service. Souls were saved like I'd never seen. Even the police would come by and tell us, "Whatever you are doing, keep doing it!" I worked with this ministry for 12 years and I loved the move of God. My daughter, grandchildren and nieces all joined this church and the Lord was moving mightily. My family was so blessed by this ministry. My nieces and nephews were saved, sanctified and Holy Ghost-filled. It was an amazing time in the Lord.

The last two years that I was with this ministry, the head pastor took over. Once in service, as the pastor was preaching, I could see that something wasn't right. I didn't quite understand what I was seeing, but my spirit was very discomforted. The sermons began to change and the spirit was not moving as it had before. Pastor Cruz began to retreat and withdraw from the members. I was no longer allowed to speak with her, but rather was encouraged to first make an appointment. This was distressing to me but I followed the new protocol. At some point, I noticed that the miracles were not flowing as they once had, and there seemed to be a strange spirit within the sanctuary.

The sermons were now geared towards denouncing witchcraft and the casting out of demons. There were things that I did not agree with, but I could do nothing about them. The pastor began to exercise a spirit of control over the entire congregation, and because she could not control me, she would say, "Sis. Nichols has a spirit that you can't handle."

The congregation would pray and start the service, but once the pastor made her arrival, things changed. I would feel a strange spirit in the church. The congregation would begin to worship her, as opposed to worshiping God. I could clearly see the spirit of mind control and manipulation. I was being quietly pushed to the background but I continued to follow the rules. At one time in particular, she began to rebuke a group of members—including my daughter—when the power of God came upon me and

I began to speak in WAR tongues! She said, "That is the Holy Ghost, I can't do nothing with that!" The power of God shut her mouth, and she couldn't say anything.

I had brought many children and adults to that church. Most of the ones who were there were ones that I had taken there. God has given me a heart after souls. One Sunday, each member was asked to invite guests. The one who brought in the most guests would win a prize. I invited a total of 146 guests, so you know I won the prize. I was with that church 100 percent, as I am with every church God sends me to.

I didn't work during the summer of 2004. "Here I go again," I said to myself. "I am going to seek God this summer." I was standing outside the church when Pastor Cruz came outside. I began to talk to her about my children's graduation, and her son speaking at the ceremony. He had been speaking at my children's 8th grade graduations for the previous five years.

She became really angry and said, "You know, I do not want my sons speaking or playing the organ over no one. I don't know what kind of spirit they have!" I apologized and told her that I was not aware of her sitting either one of them down. The next day was Sunday. She called a meeting with me that included the Board, and her prayer team. They came against me for having her sons at the school, when she said she had sat them down. She called me a name that God would not allow me to hear. She then apologized for calling me the name, but again I didn't hear it—except that I did audibly hear her call me a witch. I listened intently to all of them talk about me for about three hours. After the meeting was over, I asked her if I could come to the prayer meeting the next morning. She told me no, and said that I should just pray at home.

I thought that was the end of that, so I went home, went into my room, laid across my bed and began to talk to God to find out what was wrong. I didn't get an answer. I fasted and prayed all of the next week, asking God to open my eyes so I could see.

Finally, on the fourth Sunday in June, I went back to church thinking that everything was alright. Pastor Cruz walked in and sent the children into another room with my daughter, for which I am so thankful. She told the members she was tired of the spirit I had, and that she was going to deal with it that day. She thought that she could break me by having the entire church talking against me. The Lord spoke to me and said, "Don't you say a word!" The members lined up and said negative things about me, such as, they couldn't pray, do the praise service, prophesy, their families wouldn't come to church because I was there, I was keeping people from coming up to get saved, etc. One of the brothers even said he dreamed that I'd died. I said, "I am not dying!" Pastor Cruz was so excited about hearing that I was supposedly going to die, that she told the people to write that down!

Finally, the Lord gave me permission to speak. I raised my hand and asked for permission to speak. I said, "I am glad you all are doing this today. If you had done this last week, I would've had a heart attack. Do not feel sorry for me, I do not feel anything." When I told them that, they all became even angrier. I sat there from 12:30 p.m. to 5:00 p.m., listening to them demean my character and good name. The brother that had the dream that I was going to die apologized after it was all over.

I have been asked time after time why I just sat there. God was proving something to both Pastor Cruz, and to me. He let her know that there was nothing she could do to control me. I was able to sit there and accept their criticism because the whole time, I just kept thinking about how much God loves me.

That Monday night, we had a church dinner so I went. We had a guest speaker, and when she walked in, she said, "The devil is in this place!"

Pastor Cruz next shouted loudly, "There is a witch in here." They all clapped and hollered aloud. After the speaker finished her message, Pastor Cruz stood up and began to speak. She looked at me, shook her finger at me and said, "You will never touch my kids again."

I asked myself, "What did I do to her kids?" I said, "God, if you are with me, let that Sister who just got through speaking come lay hands on me right about now!" I was not sure if I was going to take it anymore. The speaker came over as soon as I asked God to do it. She laid hands on me and declared, "God is going to use you mightily!" Pastor Cruz heard her and did not say another word about me. As I walked out of the door, the Lord said, "Don't you go back there anymore." I have never gone back since. I asked God why didn't He tell me to leave that church sooner. God said, "Because of the love you had for the leader and the ministry, you wouldn't have believed it was Me, so that was the only way I could get you out." I am so happy that they pushed me to my destiny. Look how long it took me to get here, but I thank God for His love for me, and that I am chosen.

After this experience, I left that particular church, but my daughter and nieces and my grandchildren remained, which was the beginning of the CULT. One day, my daughter told me that she needed to leave her apartment upstairs because God's judgment was on me and she would face the same judgment if she stayed. I didn't understand what was happening, but the Lord let me know. It was a spirit of control, which is witchcraft. The more involved she became with that particular church, the further she drew away from me. I would send her money and she would send it back. I prayed and asked God to release my child. I cried and wept as any mother would. My child was distant, she withdrew away from me as her mother and drew closer to that church. I continued to call her and pray for her to no avail. My daughter and granddaughter drew farther away from me and did not speak with me for five years. I still can't believe this happened.

I continued to pray and ask God to change the situation. One day, the Lord spoke clearly to me and said, "If you want me to handle this situation, take your hands off it completely." I said, "God, I can't do that." I gave it another thought, and then I said, "God, You take her out of my heart. But whatever You do, PLEASE, do not let the devil take her life." God took her out of my heart. I called my daughter and explained that I would no longer be calling, nor sending her money. I explained to her that I had given the issue to God and that the next time she heard my voice again, it would be because she called me. I said goodbye and hung up the telephone. God took the hurt away, and removed the pain of my daughter's rejection from my heart.

▪ THE RECOVERY PROCESS ▪

After leaving the church where I experienced such grief, I began to seek the Lord and He sent me to another small church which was similar in mission. The pastor of this church was an old friend named Mother Dorothy Clark. The Lord said to me, "Go there until I tell you differently." I was a bit reluctant, but the Lord released me to stay under her watch care. I studied the Word with her, discussed what I'd gone through and talked about my hurt and pain. She would go into the Word of God and show me the Scriptures that would begin the process of my healing.

I didn't understand it then, but it is clear to me now; the Lord used a woman pastor as the vehicle to heal the pain that another woman pastor had brought into my heart. This was the Hand of the Lord. Under this pastor, the Lord healed me.

After seven years of estrangement from my daughter, Carmella, who was still a part of the church where I experienced so many issues, I received a call from my her. She said she was having stomach pains and had been admitted to the hospital. She asked if I would come. I initially did not want to go, but the Lord released me to see about her. My daughter was under so much stress, and because of it she'd begun to have seizures. When I first laid eyes upon my daughter, she was in such agonizing pain and misery. She had been diagnosed with cancer. After her surgery, I sat in the room with her. I felt bad, but not as badly as I thought I should have. I asked God, "Shouldn't I feel really sad?" God replied to my spirit, "I've got it, so why would you worry?" I felt a peace in my spirit and I stayed all night with my daughter. The Lord allowed her to have a successful operation and all of the cancer was removed. It has been over six years since now, and she has had no recurring problems.

Now once again, Carmella was still connected to the church, but continued to reach for me. I knew that God was working things out. Shortly after my daughter's successful surgery, her pastor was diagnosed with a terminal illness and passed away a few months later. After her death, my daughter left the church for good. She told me that she loved me and began to draw closer to me. For her, the issue was difficult but she knew that turning against her mother was not proper. She showed genuine daughterly love for me and prayed for total freedom.

I was free in my spirit because I knew that the allegations that were brought against me were untrue.

Carmella relocated to Oviedo, Florida, got herself a good job, married and God blessed her with the most beautiful baby. Her two older children are saved, and going on with the Lord. I hear from my daughter almost every day. My granddaughter, Denina, moved on and got married also. She and her husband just opened up a church, and God is moving mightily in their lives. Why was I forced to endure all of that angst, drama and pain? "And we know that God causes everything to work together for the good of those who love God, and are called according to his purpose for them (Romans 8:28, NLT)."

Once, while at Mother Clark's Church, Prophet Gillard from Florida came to speak. The date was August 22, 2004. I had not seen him before, nor had he seen me. He walked over to me and said these words: "You know how you put your hand into hot water and it begins to go from warm to hot? As I began to walk toward this sister (Mother Nichols), I felt like I was walking in warm water and have gotten overheated. It's the presence of the Lord that's in your life; that's the Holy Spirit and it draws people to you, because of your kindness and your love."

He continued, "I see you in the spirit of the Lord. It looks like people are lined up at your house to see you, but yet the people are sitting there and you are talking to them. You've got your hand on their heads. You are counseling the people! And, people are waiting to see you. I see you anointing your telephone, and you are speaking the Word of God, and it is going down into the line, and it is touching the people. I hear the Lord say, 'yea my daughter I've not brought you out to sit down, but I'm bringing you out and off of your job so you can minister my Word and work for me.'"

He went on to say, "In the vision, my servant saw how you are working in the minds of the people that were lined up waiting to see thee. I say unto thee, I shall touch thee in a great way, and confrontation shall spring up out of thy voice and you shall work in the hearts and minds of people. The hand on the folks' heads are five fingers, representing the five-fold ministry. Yes, the apostle mantle shall fall upon thee and shall reestablish them," said God. "Yes, a prophetic ministry shall fall upon thee and you shall go places counseling, go into homes counseling, go 'round about counseling, yea' even a pastoral anointing. You shall minister to people, and be able to babysit people. A teaching ministry shall fall upon thee and you will tell them to go to that Scripture, running reference. Be not afraid. I will raise thee up and you shall go many places," said God. "Oh, my daughter! You shall one day look upon the television set and see thine own face," said the Lord.

I received the prophecy, but wondered to myself when exactly God was going to do this. After six months with Mother Clark, the Lord revealed to me that my time there was over. I left her ministry, but little did I know that I was on my way to my destiny!

CHAPTER FIVE

CONCLUSION

▪ REWARDS ON EARTH ▪

I next visited a church which was led by a young man named Pastor John Hannah. I remembered him as a young man from St. James, so he knew who I was. As Pastor Hannah was preaching, I felt comfortable, but was not certain that this was the home church God wanted for me. During the service, I asked the Lord to show me a sign that this was my church. I asked God to allow the pastor to hold my hand. Shortly thereafter, as Pastor Hannah was preaching, he walked down the aisle, reached out and held my hand. I was excited, but still not convinced that this was to be my church home.

I visited again, and asked the Lord for one more sign. During the sermon, the pastor asked for two chairs and called out my name. He said, "Sis. Nichols, the Lord said for you to intercede for me as I preach." I did just that. He went a bit further and asked me to assist him as he prayed for the people. I was extremely comfortable at that point and knew that God had ordered my steps under the leadership of Pastor John Hannah. I was overjoyed to become a member of the New Life Covenant Church! God spoke to me and said, "I sent you there to cover Pastor Hannah." I have now been covering him since December 2004.

As a new member, I would talk to a few people, but not very many. I developed a close relationship with a young lady named Cynthia Chamberlain, who could relate to me in some ways. She and I had a beautiful friendship and I would often tell her about what happened to me. Cynthia frequently spoke encouraging words to me. She would sometimes say, "Sis. Nichols, we are not going to talk about this today, because it was just too much!" I always felt better whenever we would talk. Cynthia and I would openly laugh together and eventually, the subject would change. Although I was healed, there was still a bit of residue left in my heart. When I would talk about what happened in the past, I would begin to feel a little sad and hurt all over again because, at that time, my children were still in that CULT. Once, during the opening of a service, Pastor Hannah asked everyone to hug one another and show love. My First Lady—Anna Hannah—came over to me and held me close. She said nothing at all, just hugged me. I broke down and cried like I'd never cried before. I had never told her anything about my church hurt, but that hug was just what I needed. It was a little better after that, because I'd told her everything. Boy, was she surprised! She said to me, "I knew it was something, but figured that you would tell me in your own time." The hug Lady Anna gave me cleared the residue that was left inside me. To God be the glory, I was free!

On the 4th Sunday in June of 2008, Pastor Hannah ordained me as one of the associate pastors of New Life Covenant Church. It just amazes me how God works because exactly four years earlier, the 4th Sunday in June 2004, I sat in another church where I was accused of being possessed with demons, and working as a witch. God's timing is simply amazing! Here it was four years later to the day and I was being ordained as an associate pastor, healed, delivered from hurt, set free and ready to continue the work God had assigned to my hands.

▪ IT ALL WORKS FOR GOOD ▪

In the capacity of associate pastor, I was called upon to counsel, pray and anoint parishioners as Pastor Hannah led. I remember once, when I was working on a computer, the Lord spoke clearly to me. He said, "I have chosen you to help deliver my people, and I'm going to take you to another level in me because you have been faithful." I heard His voice so clearly until I had to write it down. A few months later, Pastor Hannah ordained me as "Pastor Nichols." The Lord spoke again and told me to pray for Pastor Hannah before his time to speak. I began praying for him with a few of the leaders and before long, several of the pastors and ministers would follow. Today, I still serve in the capacity of lead Prayer Warrior for Pastor Hannah prior to each service. God sent me to New Life as a covering for Pastor Hannah. For this, I am forever grateful.

As I look back over my life, I never would have thought that I would be in the place that I am. I never could quite understand why God would choose me for such an amazing work. A young girl who witnessed abuse, was abused, never had close friends and never really thought of myself in a great way? Why would God use me? How in the world could God chose me to work in the capacity of a pastor? One thing I always knew, however, was that God loves me. I knew this because He always watched over me and comforted me. I am honored to serve God's people and I will never really understand why God chose me.

Although I don't comprehend it, I know that God was working things out for my good. Romans 8:28 says, "And we know that all things work together for good to them that love God, to them who are the called according to his purpose (KJV)." I am a living example that God used my life to work for good. He has allowed me to share my testimony of His love, hope and miracle-working power. God has allowed me to not only witness His miracles, but I am also a benefactor!

▪ THE MIRACLES I'VE WITNESSED ▪

I am blessed to have witnessed so many miracles in my lifetime. Each of my children have seen the miracles of God. I remember when my husband was driving with our two daughters one day, somehow, the car door flew open and Brenda, just two years old at the time, fell out onto Chicago's busy Eisenhower Expressway. My husband jumped out of the car – with the car still moving – grabbed Brenda from the middle of the roadway, placed her on the grass and ran back to the car, which was about to impact with on-coming traffic. He brought my five-year old daughter, Denise, back to safety. Denise smiled, and with childlike innocence, said, "It was fun riding in the car with no one driving!" That was a laugh for everyone there. When he was coming back, Brenda had started walking back across the expressway. The police arrived and called him "Superman" because no one was hurt, and the car was intact. That was a sure miracle! On that morning, at around 8:30, I felt a very sad feeling and did not have any idea that I was about to potentially lose my entire family. "GOD, I THANK YOU, BECAUSE YOU ARE SO FAITHFUL!!

I always ask God to warn me before things happen. He always has. Sometimes, I do not know what the warning is for until it happens.

Another miracle I witnessed was with Brenda. After several tests, a doctor discovered that Brenda had fibroid tumors. The diagnosis was that one was in her uterus canal, and her chances of one day getting pregnant were low. After waiting two years, she decided to have surgery. The surgery was scheduled for March 26, 1997, but on March 19, it showed she was pregnant so the surgery was canceled. The doctors recommended that she should have a Cesarean section, owing to the fibroids.

During her 14th week of pregnancy, Brenda began having bad pains because of the fibroids. She was married for five years and had told the Lord that she wanted a child. Just as God did it for me, He did it for her. She became pregnant with a beautiful baby girl, but as the baby grew, the fibroid tumors grew. She carried the baby to full term but endured much pain. The doctor stated he was surprised Brenda was pregnant, because her cervix was tilted. She was taking pain pills, but her pains were so bad that the doctor suggested an abortion, to which she emphatically said "no." The saints were praying for her.

The Lord spoke to me and said if that would have been someone else, you would have gone over to her and prayed. I told God I would go that Friday when I left work. I went to my daughter, and we prayed. On the morning of June 1, at 2:00, she was yet in bad pain. On this particular morning, she received a visit from an angel named "Gilmore." When she lightly awakened, the man was sitting on the edge of the couch in her room, and he told her he'd come to bring her RELIEF. Gilmore stayed with her until 8:00 a.m. Brenda woke up around two times, and Gilmore again would only state his name and say, "I come to bring you RELEIF." He stayed by her side until he himself became tired, and departed.

This was the first night since the pain began that Brenda was able to sleep all through the night. Sometimes, the pains were so great that she would be up the entire night, but look at God! On the afternoon of June 1, she had her last pain and it was the worst. My Brenda said that this was the last attempt the devil tried, to convince her to abort her baby. That was the last pain. At the end of 34 weeks and 6 days, at 2:30 p.m., the pains began again, but this time they were bearable. Brenda only had one more bad pain episode before the baby was born, October 15, 1997 at 7:49 p.m. And, she did not deliver Janay Brianna by C-section.

Janay, means "God has answered," and Brianna, "to be born." She and her husband had a healthy baby girl who has grown up to be one wonderful young lady who loves God. She today is in her second year of college, studying to be a doctor. God worked a miracle for Brenda, and I witnessed it.

God worked another miracle for our son, Eugene "Nicky." At the age of three, he became extremely ill and the doctors did not know what was wrong. God whispered to me, "Take him to Bishop Campbell, and take your husband too." God wanted my husband to see the miracle. We called, and went. Bishop prayed for him, and told him to say, "thank you, Jesus" three times, but he would not say it. Bishop said, "Take him home and have him say, "Thank you, Jesus" three times, and he will be fine. When we got home, Eugene was put into bed, and I said to my son, "say Thank you, Jesus!" He said it three times and that sickness went away, and never returned! God healed him.

At the age of 38, my son had chest pains and was told that he had a displaced artery. The doctors were amazed that he was still living because the pulmonary artery (an artery in which blood travels directly from the lung to the heart) was lodged between two main arteries. He underwent over seven hours of heart surgery and the doctors performed corrective surgery. God worked another miracle for my son, and I witnessed it. The surgery was said to encompass about four hours, and because this was the first time the surgeon had performed this kind of sur gery, he was going to see if he could correct it. The surgeon further explained that God had guided his hands and he repaired it like it was supposed to have been in the first place. At one point, the artery stopped working. I always wondered if that was the time I had a feeling that something was wrong, at around 10:30 a.m. I went into the chapel and prayed until I knew something had broken, and a deep sense of peace came over me. Out of everything my son has gone through, look at him now! "TO GOD BE THE GLORY."

I've seen God work miracles for me as well. I remember being diagnosed with a skin disorder where my hands and other parts of my body were turning white. The doctors said that the disorder would travel throughout my entire body. I would put make-up on my hands because of the rapid discoloration. I wanted God to work a miracle for me and heal me. I received prayer by Bishop Mitchell. He anointed my hands and believed that God would heal me. The pigmentation disorder dissolved and God healed me totally and completely. I am a living miracle.

Once, after I had gallbladder surgery, I was doing well until all of a sudden I began to feel really sick, so I laid down in my bed. I didn't know why, but I gently laid my hands across my breast and began to drift away. The Holy Ghost spoke in my spirit and said, "No, not now! GET UP!" I knew that I was dying, but I got out of bed, immediately fell to my knees and began to pray. "When I'd made connection with God, the spirit said GET UP and get your Word. I grasped my Bible and began to read.

"There is power in the Word." I would walk and say, "God, your Word says…" and read the Scriptures. These are the last two Scriptures I read: Isaiah 41:10 –"Fear thou not; for I am with thee: be not dismayed; for I am thy God: I will strengthen thee; yea, I will help thee; yea, I will uphold thee with the right hand of my righteousness." I read another Scripture, Psalms 118:17, which says: "I shall not die, but live, and declare the works of the LORD."

After reading this Scripture, I felt like nothing had happened! The Lord said, "Now rebuke fear and death out of your house!" I began to rebuke all of the fear and death out of my house. The Lord delivered me from death. I am a miracle, and that was 19 years ago.

During one Sunday night service, Bishop Mitchell had stated, "There is someone here who has a condition in their body and God is going to heal them tonight." I stood up, and the Lord said to me: "I am going to heal you tonight, and you will have more children."

Bishop laid his hand on me, I felt a cut on my stomach, and a hand inside of my stomach. I said, "OH MY God" I am hurting worse than I was before I came up here." The Lord said, "Praise me!" I began to praise God and the saints joined me. God did a supernatural operation on me that night. I felt the cut, and I felt the pain. The next day, I came home for lunch. I had not had a cycle in 10 years, but it began once more when I came home. I called the doctor because I was not sure of what had happened. My husband reminded me that I had got in the prayer line that Sunday night. I stayed in bed for three days. I was completely healed and a year later I had a baby girl, "Carmella Yvette Nichols." Oh what a joy! WHAT A JOY IT WAS TO RAISE THAT BABY.

My husband later came to be diagnosed with Parkinson's disease and dementia. As I was standing in church in 2009, the Lord told me, "I've got to take him." I began to cry, and as I looked around, Evangelist Alma Lyons was standing close beside me, praying. I was shocked because I was wondering how she got there so fast. When I got home, I called her and asked her. She said, God said "Go to her, right now." After being home for a while, I phoned the children to let them know what God had said. We were all sad. We prayed for God to heal, but he assured us that that was not His will. I asked for more time, and God gave us six more years! The Word said if you ask anything in His name and don't doubt it, He will do it. As his illness progressed, he would get up at night, go outside, leave the house and pack up to move. I began to pray and talk to God. I said, "God! This is too much. I can't handle this." The Lord said it was nothing but a spirit. I began to pray and bind every spirit that was not right, and that kept tormenting him. Afterward, he began to calm down and I was able to function normally. God said, "I give you power over every spirit."

On a particular evening, I was so tired that I went to the bedroom and locked the door behind me. My husband came and knocked on the door. The Spirit said to me, "Do not open that door." He knocked again, walked away for a little while and came back to see if he could turn the knob. He said, "You do not have to have these two big men at the door."

I laid down for a little while longer. I opened the door and he was standing in the middle of the floor, shaking like a leaf on a tree, he was so afraid. I asked him what he was doing. He said, "I was trying to see if you were in the room."

I said, "No, you were doing something else."

Then he said, "I was trying to open that door, and that man said don't you touch that knob." Angels of the Lord, I thought to myself! I was covered. He came again and repeated the same thing. The next time he came, he ventured just halfway down the hall before going back and sitting down. God's word is true! I WONDER WHAT MY HUSBAND WAS THINKING!

On September 3, 2015, he went to the doctor. The Lord told me that he wouldn't be back. As my husband's illness got worse, he ceased eating. The doctors wanted to put a tube in his stomach, but God said "no." The doctors wanted to put the tube in right away, the very next day. I had to sign the papers. The doctor who told me that the tube was urgently necessary walked in one day with another physician. The new doctor said, "I hate to come in like this, but why do you want to have him suffering more? You don't know if that tube is going to help him, nor do you know if they'll be able to do anything about the bedsores."

I said, "You mean I do not have to make a hasty decision?" He said, "No, take all the time you want." The doctor who said, "right away" asked: "What do I do?" The new doctor replied, "cancel it." He walked out and I did not see him anymore (the Angel of the Lord).

I got ready to leave and the Lord told me to pray for my husband. I prayed for him as the Lord had said. He began to chew as I was praying. I asked the nurse, "Will you test him again?" She said, "sure!" I went home and returned the next day at noon. At 12:10 p.m., they brought some food in. He ate a small amount. I said, "Shouldn't he eat more?" The nurse said, "He is still full. He ate all of his breakfast, toast, grits, sausage, a sweet roll and he drank all of his milk." Before the tube could be placed, my husband ate a full meal! This simply amazed the doctors. God was with us even in sickness. My children cared for their dad day and night for the nearly six years, until the Lord took him home to heaven. God granted my request and gave me more time with him. Before he passed away, the Lord said, "Why do you want to keep him here suffering? I can take him home, and take care of him better than you can." God took him home on December 1, 2015. I am looking forward to seeing him again. We were married for 59 wonderful years. I knew that God was in control and would take care of us all.

My goodness, I am so excited that God loves me. He proves His love each and every day. I'm in love with Jesus, and He's in love with me! God did not allow me to grieve not even one day. He said, "Why would I bring you this far, and leave you?"

Grieving is a spirit. I pray for everyone who is grieving and cannot seem to control it, in the name of Jesus. I bind that spirit in Jesus' name, and send it to dry places. Amen.

▪ GOD'S LOVE FOR LOVIE ▪

God has been amazing to me, and I thank Him every day. At nearly 80 years old, I can see how God's love brought me through so much. I have seen many things throughout my lifetime, and I have experienced God's hand at every turn of my life. He has never failed me. Even though the devil has tried to stop my testimony, God gave me the strength to endure and stay the course. It was never easy. However, God's love pushed me and at my weakest times, He carried me.

I remember counseling someone a while back, who was pregnant out of wedlock. She shared the details with me of how she'd recently met a man and became pregnant with his child. I was a bit disturbed because I was thinking, this does not sound good. That night, the Lord revealed to me that my mother only knew my father for one week when she became pregnant with me. He asked, "Were you a mistake? LOOK AT WHAT I DID WITH YOU!"

Wow! The way it happened was a sin, but children are an inheritance from the Lord. I was able to use my own personal experience to help this young lady. She has identical twins, and is extremely blessed to this day.

▪ STAY THE COURSE ▪

No matter what comes your way, you must stay the course because God has a plan for your life. If God did it for me, he can do it for you. Be encouraged and stay the course. It will work out for your good in the end. "Remember, God is not a man that He should lie; neither the son of man, that he should repent; hath he saith, and shall he not do it? Or hath he spoken, and shall he not make it good (Numbers 23:19)."

OPEN YOUR BIBLE, READ IT AND BELIEVE WHAT IT SAYS. THE WORD IS GOD, TALKING TO YOU.

In 2014, God told me to start a prayer line. I did as instructed, and it runs from 5:30 to 6:30 a.m., Monday through Friday. People are being healed, delivered and set free, and so much more. It reaches as many as 180 homes on some mornings.

▪ MY PRAYER ▪

"Father, God, in the name of Jesus, I thank You for allowing me to write this book. I pray that those who read this book, and those I come into contact with will be delivered and set free. God, You said You called and chose me to help deliver Your people. Father, I pray that a special anointing will come upon me to pray and counsel Your people. Lord, use me to touch the lives of others, and show me what You want me to do to be a blessing to Your people. Help me to make a big difference in the world for Your glory. Father, my greatest treasure is in serving You. In Jesus' name, AMEN!"

● ● ● ●

CHAPTER SIX

IN THEIR OWN WORDS
▪ WHO PASTOR NICHOLS IS TO ME ▪

Family first...

Denise Chambers (first daughter)

I was asked by my mom to write something about her to add to her book. My thoughts went to so many things. I thought about my upbringing and how my mom and dad always wanted what was best for my siblings and I. My mom knew the importance of having a good education, and she wanted us to have the best one possible. We went to some of the best high schools and colleges in the Chicago area and are now living successful lives. She was careful to not allow us to be exposed to negative influences. She always taught us what was right and lived the life before us. Most importantly, my mom taught us to love the Lord and to live our lives so that it pleased God.

She prayed and interceded on our behalf continually. It is because of my mom's prayers that I am saved today, and I myself intercede on behalf of my children. My mom was, and still is a strong and dominant woman. Her powerful influence in my life has truly shaped who I am today. I know she will always be there for me and I know that I can always call upon her whenever I need her. She is my advisor, my counselor, my intercessor and my friend. But most of all, she is my mom and I love her. Congratulations mom, may God shower His blessings upon you now and forever. I love you!

Brenda Nichols-Taylor (second daughter)

I am Pastor Nichols' second child. She worked days and daddy worked nights. I really appreciate how they made sure a parent was always there with us. When my daughter was born, my mother and my father were happy to watch my daughter. I really appreciate that they were able to do that. My mother has always been someone I felt I could talk to about anything. My mother has always been there for me, and supported me in the things I've wanted to do. She is truly a Prayer Warrior. I could always count on her to get a prayer through when needed. Love you, Mom.

Eugene Nichols (son)

Mama, I am so proud of you. What a major accomplishment. You have written a book that not only captures your life story, but will also serve as inspiration and encouragement to so many. There are points in this book that I was not even aware of. Your book makes even more clear why you are such an amazing mother.

You are a mother of great strength, determination and persistence, but more importantly, an unwavering lover of GOD. Your love for GOD and example of what a life for Christ looks like, is the reason I and the rest of your children (my sisters) are saved today. Thank you for your love for GOD. Thank you or praying for me when I didn't even know it. And, thank you for being present and involved during my formative years. Because of your standards, your qualities, your character and your prayerful life, I am the man that I am today.

I love you so much. I wish you long life and pray that your latter years continue to be greater than your former.

Love, your only son (LOL), Eugene

Carmella Nichols (third daughter)

My mom, Lovie Nichols, is the best mom anyone could ever have. Growing up, I've never quite understood certain things we were taught to do as Christians, but I obeyed. When I became older, I saw the benefits and realized how living for God the way we did growing up taught me a lot. I lived my life but I wasn't perfect, and I took my mom through it at times. She always forgave me, prayed for me and walked with me every step of the way. I know God to be a healer.

I love my mom more than she'll ever know for teaching me what it means to have faith and trust in God, no matter what the circumstances look like. I'm the woman I am today from having a mother who is powerful, anointed and full of wisdom. I now have two daughters and one son. I've raised them to live for God and to know that every part of their lives must represent Him. May God continue to bless you. Love you, mom.

Dr. Darlene Allen-Nichols (daughter in-law)

Mother Lovie Nichols is my God-mother and mother-in-love. I have been married to her son since 1996, and Mom Nichols has been a staple in my life since childhood. She is a woman of power, authority, grace, strength and amazing courage. My biological mother passed away in June of 2015, and Mom Nichols stepped up to the plate to serve as my role model and a strong voice of reason and strength for me. Her wisdom is undeniable, her anointing is overwhelming and her power is amazing. I am forever grateful for the connection with Mom Lovie Nichols, and thank God for placing this jewel in my life.

Congratulations on your book, Mom!

Deja Craig (grandchild)

There are a lot of things I love about my grandma. I don't have time to tell it all, but I will tell you that the most favorite thing I love about her is her faith in God, and how passionate she is about her walk with God. Her relationship with God has challenged me to do better in my relationship with Him. She is so persistent in her prayers, that it's amazing. The way she keeps trusting God even when things got tough is really what I will never forget about her. She's selfless, and puts others before herself. I hope to be half the woman she is. I love her to death! And I don't know what I would do without her! Love you grandma!

Deion Craig (grandchild)

Lovie Nichols is my Grandmother. My grandma is one of the most important, caring, loving and outgoing people I know. I do not know where I would be without my grandma in my life. Any time I need something or someone to just talk to, she is always there. She is also one of the most powerful women of God I know. I am so blessed to be able to call her my grandma, and she is a mom and grandma to so many others. I'm so honored to have her as a grandma and I know she is always praying for me. I love her so much!

Denina Flowers (grandchild)

My mother is Eugenia Chambers. She is the first born of Lovie Nichols, and I am the eldest grandchild of Lovie Nichols. My grandmother has been around for my entire life. I remember when I was younger, spending time at my grandmother's house on the West Side of Chicago. We would eat Sunday dinners at her house. Her salmon patties, rice and biscuits were the best. I remember the games we played with the neighborhood kids, especially the time spent with my aunt Carmella.

Growing up, I used to think my grandmother was mean, but as I got older, I realized that she was stern. The Bible says to raise up a child in the way they should go, and when they get older, they will not depart from it. My grandmother raised my mother, who in turn raised us to fear God and trust His word. I know that because of the prayers of my mother and grandmother, I am the woman I am today!

When I was 22, I was at a place in my life where I thought I was going to lose my mind. Nothing made sense. I wanted to end my life and end the life of my husband (now ex-husband). I had a dream that I needed a doctor. My grandmother happened to call me, and I told her about the dream. She pointed me to doctor Jesus! She invited me to church. That Sunday, I accepted the Lord as my personal savior and was filled with the Holy Ghost with the evidence of speaking with other tongues. I have been going for the Lord ever since.

We were in a ministry together for years, which was actually a cult. At the time, I did not know. I was blind, and only did what the pastor said. In the midst of it, my grandmother left the ministry. I cut her and my other family out of my life. It was a horrible feeling to not have my family, but I thought I was doing right. I prayed! My grandmother prayed for me consistently, even when I refused to speak to her. It wasn't until about five years ago that we began to speak again. God brought me out! I asked my grandmother and family to forgive me. The awesome thing is they forgave me as Jesus forgave me. I know the reason I am free today is because of the prayers of my mother and grandmother. I cannot thank them enough for what they have done for me.

Now, I am 36 years old with three beautiful children, married to a man of God who preaches God's Holy Word and most importantly, I am SAVED!!! Thank you, grandma! I Love You!

"Therefore, my dear brothers and sisters, stand firm. Let nothing move you. Always give yourselves fully to the work of the Lord, because you know that your labor in the Lord is not in vain (1 Cor. 15:58 (NIV)."

Brittany Jones (grandchild)

My name is Brittany Jones. I am 21 years old and Lovie Nichols is my grandmother. Through Grandma Lovie, I have learned the incredible power of unwavering dedication, faith and optimism. I have learned to always keep it real, and to never be intimidated. While she may have never sat me down and physically taught me these attributes, her actions have said enough. She has instilled within my mother, and therefore me, values that serve as a recipe for a powerful woman.

Grandma Lovie embodies the true meaning of a Christian woman, and for that reason she is highly favored. She is not only highly favored by God, but by her family as well. In accordance with human genetics, I have 25 percent of Grandma Lovie's genes. Therefore, to me, Grandma means that I, too, will be powerful and highly favored.

Jennifer Jones (grandchild)

Grandmother is defined as the mother of one's father or mother. However, my grandmother means more than that to me. She is the mother of our family. She is the thread that keeps it all together. Our intercessor to speak to God on our behalf, but more so teaching me how to intercede on my own behalf.

My grandma has been the model of a good wife, a loving mother, a teacher, a praying grandmother and a Prayer Warrior. My grandma has been my savior when I didn't know I needed saving. To me, my grandmother means the world, but she is also this for so many others. She lends her home, heart and ears to those in need and gives direction to those who may be lost.

My grandmother has been someone I could always count on to never change. She will be there when she says she will, but won't be afraid to tell you "no." She is the one I can go to for advice about anything— relationships, friendships, life, etc.—and know that the answers will be the unfiltered truth.

She is a lover of the Lord and an inspiration to me. She spoke to the devil a long time ago and made it known he had no room to dwell within our family, and her faith has never wavered. She trusts and believes God will continue to protect and keep us all. It has been those very prayers that saved me from my own bad decisions, and saved our family in our lowest and weakest moments. My grandmother is the strongest woman I know. She is unbreakable, and immovable. My grandmother is who I one day wish and hope to be like. To possess a faith that knows without a doubt that it can move mountains, to know that life is all in God's hands and nobody can change that, to trust that God never fails...

What does my grandma mean to me? She means everything!

Larry Jones (grandchild)

A grandmother is the root of a family. We utilize our grandmothers for knowledge, guidance, support, a good meal and so much more. One thing that most grandmothers are often sought out for is prayer! I can attest to that being my grandmother's greatest trait. Lovie Nichols is a Prayer Warrior and Holy soldier. I have never been in a situation that she couldn't pray me out of! My life has had some ups and some downs, but at the age of 27 with all that I have including my daughter, fiancé and a well-paying career in corporate America, I can only attribute my success in life to first off God, and second, my grandmother's prayers!

Sherridon Lyons-Verse (niece)

Sometimes God will put a person in your life to challenge you. You call her Pastor Lovie Nichols. I call her Aunt Lovie. She is, and has been that person for me. She is the representation of a more excellent way for me. She is one of the most focused people I know. She knows what she wants, and settles for nothing less. My desire to finish high school was because I saw her instill within her own children the importance of an education.

She talked to me about the kind of life I would have, and tried to instill in me the desire to do better. Like most young people, I didn't always want to listen and we clashed for that reason. I have heard it said that, "We clash with the people we are most like. Those are the people we should study and learn from." I saw in her an example of a better way of life, and the importance of knowing God for yourself. I can say that I have learned much from her life, and I am better because of it. She is, and has been an encouragement to me.

Austin Nichols (grandchild)

I am the grandson of Lovie Nichols. I love my grandma so much, and she means the world to me. My grandmother is the best grandmother I could ever have. I am so grateful to have a grandmother like mine.

I love you grandma, Austin

Eugene Nichols, III (grandchild)

My Grandmother is a phenomenal woman. Growing up, she has always been one of my biggest supporters, and is one of the main reasons why I am the person who I am today. She fostered academic and spiritual excellence throughout all of her grandchildren, and makes it her duty to prioritize that each and every last one of us succeeds. No matter how many crazy ideas I've come up with, she's been right there with me every step of the way. Moreover, despite my decision to go to school in New York, my relationship with God has strengthened due to the online calls and constant prayers from her.

Grandma Lovie is the matriarch of our family, and is the glue that keeps us together. Without her strength and resilience to lead our family, I do not think I would be who I am today.

With Love,
Eugene Nichols, III ("EJ")

Janay Taylor (grandchild)

From the time I was born, my grandma has loved me unconditionally and I love her the same. Both my grandma and grandpa watched after me every day as my mom worked until I was old enough to be home by myself. Although I don't remember much of it, I really do appreciate both of them. No matter what, they made sure I had everything including family, fun and food! Two things I love about my grandma are her love for God and how prayerful she is. She has, and continues to make sure everyone in our family has a relationship with God. A big reason for who I am and what I have stems from the constant prayers of my grandma. I love her dearly for who she is, and the wonderful family she has created.

With love, Janay♥

Jamela Ward (grandchild)

Iam Jamela, and what my grandmother means to me is hope. Hope for the next day, hope for prayer, hope for a healthy life. She encourages me to have hope in God. She encourages me to stay strong. She encourages me to live my life to the fullest. Every time I'm in the hospital or feeling discouraged, she is always there, praying for me to have faith and now there is no doubt in my mind that God will always be there for me. Thanks to my grandmother, I believe in myself and in God.

Farrah Lloyd (grandchild)

What my Grandmother means to me is loving and faithful. She means faith to get me through the day; she gives me strength to keep going when I'm tired of going back and forth from hospitals, but I never gave up because she was always there to pick me up when I fell. She is someone I can call on anytime of night. No matter if we are right or wrong, my grandmother stands by her grandchildren. My Grandmother always has many great words of encouragement to push us to be better. From a young age, she taught me to put God first in all that I do and to know that He must always be the head of my life. My Grandmother is my angel. She always looks out for me when I get discouraged and pulls me through the storm. I love my Grandmother and I thank her for everything she's done for me. Without her, I don't know what I would have done. She taught me everything I know about having faith and being strong. She's helped me reach my path of righteousness.

Love you, Farrah
In Their Own Words

A tribute from friends and mentees...

Minister Andrea Alexander

My encounter with the wonderful Pastor Nichols began at King High School of Chicago. I had heard that she was a school teacher, so I slid beside her and sat for a minute, knowing that she was praying. Then, I asked her if she was a school teacher. She nodded, so I asked her if she could tutor me in English. She responded yes, and then went on to ask me where I lived, because you know she doesn't like driving at night! This began our relationship of me driving for her.

So, after a long period of time, I asked her again when are you going to tutor me? She looked at me and said, "I don't do any tutoring." I went there, and reminded her of our conversation. She then stated that she was praying to God to send her someone who could drive her at night, and started laughing. That's has been close to 13 years ago. I've been tutored in something much better than English, though. Pastor Nichols has been my Angel, she covers me in prayer, supports my endeavors and reminds me to say what I mean, and mean what I say. Furthermore, how to forgive. They call her Mother Nichols. She has really been a mother to me. Spiritual and physical. She has so much love for people.

Loretta Allen

Dear Pastor Mother Lovie Nichols, what a unique and precious jewel YOU are! Words cannot express how grateful I am that the Holy Spirit has divinely connected us together.

You not only are a woman of prayer, and a woman with the gift of faith, you are very humorous as well! Thank you for just being YOU.

Pastor Mother Nichols, you share so much of yourself with so many that you may not even know the indelible impact you have been. You have been an advisor, an ambassador of the truth, a comedian, a faith builder and a friend. We trust and believe that the love that God has for "Lovie," will cause others to thirst after, desire and seek for the love of Christ, through this book. Gratefully yours,
Loretta Allen

Marlene Allen

From the time I was a child, I have known Mother Lovie Nichols. She was good friends with my mother and they talked often. One thing I have always admired about Mother Nichols is her commitment and conviction to Jesus Christ.You could always find Mother Nichols working in the church, doing whatever her hands found to do in ministry. She was always a Prayer Warrior, and stood in the gap for those who needed God.

Even as a school teacher, she quietly prayed for her students, asking God to open their minds, fix matters at home and keep the children safe. I have witnessed that she is a woman of power who has a solid relationship with Jesus Christ. She loves her family and has a great sense of humor. Mother Nichols is definitely a gift to the Body of

Christ, and I can't wait to read the many experiences she's encountered during her lifelong walk with Jesus.

Marlene Allen,
Your Spiritual Daughter

Robin Allen

Mother Nichols is the EPITOME of sanctification holiness, and a matriarch of prayer. She has been my constant partner of accountability, prayer, encouragement and faith! I've easily opened myself up to every word of sound wisdom that's uttered from her lips, to be poured into me! Mother Nichols has encouraged me in so many ways...one direct nugget from her has been, "Robin, when you open God's Word and you read it, believe what it says and God is going to do just what He says!" I'm proud of her aspiration to write this book. I wish God's continued blessings upon her!

Sonya Baine

I first encountered Pastor/Mother Nichols during the prayer before Sunday morning service. She suddenly appeared and without hesitation, in a determined, yet calm voice, said, "It's time for prayer.

Stop walking, stop talking. Devil get to crawling..." During that prayer, she talked to God just like one person talking to another. She asked God for what she expected, what He promised and told the devil what he couldn't have. Period.

I was blessed to discover that this Mighty Woman of God also led a 5:30 a.m. prayer call. As I dialed in, I was drawn to her prayers and words of wisdom. I was encouraged by her instructions on how to have faith. I was lifted by her reminders about God's promises. I was inspired by her personal testimonies and I was spiritually educated by her instructions on how to defeat the enemy. I began quoting some of Mother's wisdom on social media. Each time I was led to do so, there would be overwhelming responses from people saying they needed to hear that specific Word.

Mother always makes herself available. She loves God's people. When I face adversity, I hear Mother's voice. When I need to read God's Word, I hear Mother's voice. I love her so much. I am thrilled that God has allowed her to write a book. The world needs to hear Pastor/Mother Nichols' voice.

Crystal Barrett

I truly believe there are no words to effectively describe who Pastor Lovie Nichols is to me, nor exactly what she means to me. I will try here, however, so let's begin with the first part.

Pastor Nichols is one of my pastors at church. She is my ministry team leader, and she is the leader of the Prayer Warriors, of which I am a part. In these roles, she selflessly gives and pours into me the wisdom she has acquired. She holds me accountable and gives me a gingerly nudge of direction when it's needed (remember, ginger is a spice that can have quite a sting to it)—all for the good to make me better, so full of love and God. I never thought I could pray for more than five minutes at a time. What would I say? Now, under the direction of Pastor Nichols, my prayer life is definitely unceasing. She has nurtured and challenged me and makes sure I'm growing and on the right track.

Pastor Nichols is a pillar of holiness to me; all that is about God and His plan. Though she is not perfect, she is a diamond in my life who strives to push me (with all of my flaws) toward God, and becoming all that He created me to be.

I am honored to have Pastor Nichols as a mentor and leader in my life. What an awesome example she is of a woman of God who is definitely all about bringing souls into the Kingdom. She wants everyone to know God as their personal savior. Thank you, Pastor Nichols, for caring so much about me. I love you so much, and my goal is always to give back to you as much as you have given me. Thank God for you, all for His Glory.

Nicole Bonner Kirk

I affectionately call Lovie Nichols, "Mom." She has been like a mother to me since I met her. I lost my mother when I was nine years old. I was raised by a series of relatives, always longing to fit in. I was always searching for a mother's love. I met "Mother Nichols" and over a short time, we bonded. I adopted her and she allowed me to. I watched her, I listened to her. I sought her out, I wanted to be in her presence. Mother Nichols allowed me into her world. God had given me a mother figure.

I have been prayed for, counseled by, reprimanded, poured into and loved on by Lovie Nichols. I call upon her often, and there has never been a time that she did not make me feel like she was there for me. Mom always had the time to address my latest concern, or prayer request. I can reach her by phone, text, Facebook, Periscope, Instagram, or Marco Polo. Mom is up to date on all the latest social networking media sites. Lovie Nichols is fast with the texting also.

Lovie Nichols has a way of making things so plain. She has asked me a basic question that made me give profound thought to my entire way of thinking. I love the way she rebukes the devil. I have gained so much peace from hearing her say, "return to sender." I don't have to accept what the devil sends my way! I have been given sound Biblical advice to face challenges that I have encountered.

Although I have countless memories of her miracle-working prayers, I will share this one: I once had let a family member come to stay with me for a few months. The situation began to cause me stress. I told Mother Nichols, and we prayed. The relative left that day going to the store, and returned about six months later to retrieve their belongings and to thank me for helping them.

Mother Nichols invited me to the prayer line at its inception. I thank God that I get to hear her voice every day. When she prays for her family, I know that means me too! I am her daughter. I thank her family for sharing her with me. My children know and love her and call upon her also. Lovie Nichols is my "GODMOM!"

God picked her just for me. He knew what I needed, and I am forever thankful!

Lakesha Bright

Mother Nichols is truly a Godsend; a rare and true living angel. I have been to many churches and have met many pastors, but have never met anyone quite like her. She is dedicated, selfless, loving, compassionate and a true believer. God always sends people into our lives to bless us and to show us that His love is real. Mother is one that God sent into my life at the right time. When I met her, I was going through one of the harshest times of my life. I actually thought that my life was over. I had completely lost my faith. With barely an ounce left, I called New Life Church to speak to someone...anyone. It was Mother Nichols who called me back.

I still remember our first conversation. I shared with her a glimpse of what was going on, and she said to me,

"We are going to pray...God answers my prayers, and He will answer yours too!" Mother had enough faith for the both of us, and it didn't stop there. She held onto me and continued to lift me up in prayer. I can call her anytime and she always opens her ears and heart. She never judges, and is always ready to go into warfare prayer.

Mother Nichols is the epitome of a spiritual Mother, Prayer Warrior and loving pastor. I know Mother always gives all the glory to God. I am grateful to God for her. I am ever so grateful that Mother allows God to use her to bless countless others. She is obedient, and steadfast. I consider myself blessed and know for sure that God loves me to have sent Mother into my life! Thank you, Mother, for who you are and all that you do.

Nyna Campbell

Mother Nichols is what I affectionately call her. This woman means so much to me. We connected through my cousin/little brother, Fred Hunter. He asked us all to come pray at his school, where he would now be the new Principal. I was going through a few family related trials at the time, and asked her if I could call her and talk to her. She was very open and approachable. Much to my delight she was encouraging, very straightforward, truthful, full of the WORD of God and to my surprise, extremely funny. Mother said things so relatable to my situation. She was open and transparent about her childhood, marriage, parenting, career and her walk with Christ.

She loves the truth as God sees it. Talking to her would always calm my fears down. Mother is a woman of integrity and character who never changes. She gives me advice without being super deep. Her counsel is practical, simple and easy to digest. When I came to New Life Covenant Southeast Church, I had experienced some things and was not a strong believer in church leadership. My family was in a delicate position and I was the intercessor for my family that had lost hope. Mother spoke things into my life that instilled faith. God used her to rescue me. I was able to pray in faith again.

She helped me believe my children would be living for the Lord and that my husband would be restored. When you lose hope, you are crushed and through her making me laugh real hard sometimes, speaking the truth in love, and praying with me, I was able to get back up.

I'm glad Mother and I still have a great relationship because the trials began to increase in my family over the years. She is a faithful woman who loves deeply and is always there when I reach out. I was praying about wanting to pray with some women. I did not mention this to her. She called to invite me to pray on the prayer line with her, and other true intercessors. My oldest daughter went through a very serious trial and Mother had insight about what she was going through. She said it to me and I was able to go back and ask my daughter if that was the case, and it sure was. My daughter began to talk with Mother on the phone, and she helped her not just make it through the difficulty, but overcome it. My daughter is 23 years old. She loves Mother and always talks about how their conversations helped her.

I have a mother who is very present in my life, and whom I love dearly. Mother Nichols replaced my grandmother. God brought us together. She also allows one to see her vulnerability. She talks about her failures, hurts, desires and hopes. She tells me, and lets me pray for her. I really love this woman because she is like her name, LOVIE! She hates the devil and all of his imps! Most of all, her faith in a very real God is what impresses me most about MOTHER!

Jerome Cook

When the name Mother Nichols is mentioned, instantly what comes to mind is the word, "General." Mother Nichols has become a lifeline to me in the area of prayer and intercession.

Her love for God's people is very real. Earlier in the year, my faith was truly tested when the enemy attacked my family. The one person whom I called upon was Mother Nichols. She took the time to pray, council and encourage me. My phone would ring every hour to check on me and my family. Out of all of the people that God has assigned her, she interceded for me until I got my strength back, and my family was restored. I love you so much, Mother Nichols. I appreciate you, and thank you for sharing your life's journey.

Janet Chrisp

How awesome it is to be a yielded vessel that prays for God's beloved. How blessed you must be to be entrusted with such a huge responsibility. And the faith you must have in order to answer His call! I love you, Pastor Nichols, and I am grateful to God for your presence in my life.

You taught me to be on guard and to resist the devil daily (1 Peter 5:8-9; James 4:7), to be consistent in refusing to give him any leeway (Ephesians 4:27) and to always maintain a firm stance against his tactics by which he uses thoughts, ideas and suggestions (Ephesians 6:11).

God strategically placed me on the pew behind you at church so I could see firsthand what it looks like to fully submit and serve Him. You've shown me that it's an anointing, a gift, a divine responsibility and not a position. I've watched you advise, lay hands on and pray for God's beloved. Never in a manner to be seen, or exploit those seeking help; but always for the glory of God. As to say, devil, that's another one for Jesus.

I once was seriously going through and praying for an answer with no response. I was having a Daniel conflict in the heavenly realm. The devil was blocking my prayers. I began to ask God, "why?" That evening, you said, "I have something for you." You handed me the number for your prayer line. I asked, "How did you know?" You responded, "You are Janet, right? GOD said, JANET!" I shouted, "THANK YOU, JESUS!" I think I hugged you so tight that it made you uncomfortable.

The next day I called the prayer line, and I've been on it for over three years now. This was the key to opening doors currently closed in my life, as well as future doors that needed to be not just opened, but kicked open! Prayer has changed my life. My brother received a miracle. No more dialysis. His failing kidneys were restored to 100 percent. God gets the glory for the end results, and you get the victory for being the vessel God used so those struggling can get to their results.

You've shown me how not to be afraid to confront the devil. Your words, "I HATE THE DEVIL" bless me every time I hear you say them. Thank you for being a fierce example. No punk! You'd say "Don't let the devil run all over you. Tell the devil where to go, then open the door and kick him out. Take back your control."

Even when you lost your husband, you never stopped interceding. You exemplified how to grieve with the hope of Christ knowing our loved ones are with the Lord. With that being said, thank you, Pastor Nichols! Know that I love you! Know that you are such a blessing, and so appreciated!

Princess Davis

Mom Nichols is the epitome of beauty. God put her into my life to be my spiritual mom. I wasn't raised by my birth mother, but God always had a way of filling the void by blessing me with special women in my life such as Mom Nichols. She truly means a lot to me because I met her through prayer. What a grand way to meet someone, I would say! I hope to have a prayer life as powerful and effective as hers someday. She is truly someone legendary and I am blessed to be a part of her life. May God continue to strengthen you to continue to bless people's lives. Thank you for blessing mine. I love you, Mom.

Minister Tonette Dugar

You should never judge a book by its cover. This is indeed a true statement when it comes to Mother Nichols. I'm torn between which Mother Nichols to write about. Do I write about the no-nonsense side who says what she means and means what she says? There are no gray areas with her. Do I expound on her knowing her assignment here in the earth, which is to help deliver God's people? Should I share about her being tech-savvy and how she came to send her first text which was "I did it, Ha!" Would others be interested in knowing that she is a comedienne? Or, do I tell how if you're driving her somewhere, she will tell you the route to take and answering your phone is not allowed.

I was divinely connected to Mother Nichols during a time of transition in my life. My mother moved to another state for a time, and I had no idea how this would affect me. During that time and to this day, she has loved me like a daughter (I'm her other baby). This has not always been the coddling type of love, but there were some tough-love days that I had to endure. We have experienced distance, but never a disconnect.

Big Lovie, I am so grateful for you, and I pray the anointing of Caleb would rest upon you and that I Corinthians 2:9 would be your portion. I love you.

Minister Margeree Ellison

This is what I have seen and learned concerning Pastor Lovie Nichols. I learned that she is faithful in what God has given her to do, and will not be persuaded by other's thoughts or beliefs about her. I have seen the passion that she has for families and her faithfulness in praying for them; she is stern in her words and true to her words, as much as she can be with the help of God. I saw that she has faith in the love that God has for her. And what He has given her to do, she will do with all that's within her to bring deliverance to God's people.

Pastor Lovie has a heart of compassion which many do not see because they look at the outer appearance of her face, and do not discern her heart. She has such compassion for those that are hurting, broken and in bondage. I have learned that she will tell the truth even if it hurts her, or you, because of her love for Jesus Christ. She believes that there is nothing too hard for God. If you say you trust God, she will tell you to act like it, walk the walk and don't just talk the talk. She believes in holiness and that's obeying the Word of God.

Pastor Nichols has come through many trials and has had many encounters with God, which have taught her to hang on no matter what the cost. There is no option of giving up. She has come to my rescue at many a time, when the enemy was closing in like a flood in my life. She would always remind me of where God brought me from, and what He brought me out of, and this gave me strength.

I learned that she does not push anyone to do what they say they cannot do, but she will let you know that you can do it through God's grace.

She does not need a platform to do the will of God. She always says, "Why do it if it's not for souls? The reward comes from God. You should be able to do God's will with, or without an audience." Pastor Lovie Nichols is steadfast, and not fake nor a pretender; she is the real deal. She prays and gets answers because she knows God hears her and answers those who believe and trust in Him. If something does not happen when she prays, she goes to the source and asks the Lord "Why, what am I doing wrong, was I in unbelief, or are You saying wait?" She is a woman who loves her family very much and is always there for them. Pastor Nichols can be a good friend. It takes time to learn her ways. She is not a person who is moved by emotions or feelings, but when you do get to know her, you can call on her for anything.

Wendy Gordon

It's a great privilege and honor to write something about the awesome, powerful and wonderful woman of God that I call "Mother Lovie Nichols." Mother, my little tribute to you flows directly from my heart. You are so loved and cherished. There are not words adequate enough to describe just how important you are to me.

Everything you do in ministry is saturated with love for others. I know I have felt it many times. When I think of you, I think of love. Calling someone "Mother" identifies that person as loving and caring. How appropriate that God arranged for your name to be "Lovie." Lovie Nichols is who you are, and you have fulfilled your name wonderfully. When I started on the prayer line with you, I would write down every Scripture verse that you would bring up, and applied them to the conversation. I took it to heart, and applied it to my life. This process under your guidance has strengthened me and given me more confidence in my walk with the Lord. You have taught me what the fruit of the spirit is as expressed as a Proverbs 31 woman, because you not only taught it, you lived it.

> *"She is clothed with strength and dignity.*
> *She can laugh at the days to come.*
> *She speaks with wisdom, and is faithful.*
> *Instruction is on her tongue.*
> *She watches over the affairs of her household*
> *and does not eat the dread of idleness.*
> *Her children arise and called her blessed."*

You never stopped encouraging me, and many others to "hang in there" during difficult times, and to trust and believe in the Lord with all of our hearts. Your efforts have truly blessed me and were a primary catalyst to help me mature in Jesus. You always made yourself available, made me feel welcome and demonstrated a genuine, caring persona. Some years ago, I lost my birth mother prematurely, which created an empty spot in my soul. You have become a wonderful "mother figure" to me and filled that empty spot with your motherly love—Mother Lovie style. Simply put, Mother, you are precious to me and have made a significant difference in my life, and only eternity will reveal how important and influential it has been.

Jesus loves Mother Lovie Nichols with His perfect love, and she reflects that love to all who know her. I am glad that God brought her into my life. I love you, Mother Lovie.

Your spiritual daughter,
Wendy

Latoya Hallmon

An accountability partner who knows God and has a strong relationship with Him, Pastor Nichols has been an inspiration in my life. Now, I know why Pastor Hannah says to get an accountability partner to help you grow spiritually into knowing God personally for yourself through a relationship with Him. Pastor Nichols would say, "If I pray for you, that's one thing; but you need to learn how to pray so when you can't reach me, you know how to call on Him for yourself." Then she would ask, "Are you walking up right and living right? Ask yourself what am I doing wrong that things are not going as expected in my life? I will not sugar coat your mess." Then, I would say, "MA, just forget it, I'm fighting a losing battle." Then she would chuckle. Being set free from drug addiction reminds me that I am one step away if I don't stay around people who are wise. (Being around wise people makes you wise; being around a fool make you foolish.) Pastor Nichols taught me to stay the course and to not give in; to stop letting that devil get inside my head. I HATE THE DEVIL! I may not always agree with her methods, technique and style, but I can surely say that if it wasn't for her keeping tabs on me, I would find myself drifting in self-pity which leads to doubt, disbelief, emotional rollercoasters and other capricious habits.

Pastor Nichols, thank you for everything!

Michael Harris

Determined, steadfast, consistent, relentless, unwavering and compassionate. These are a few of the words that come to mind when Pastor/Mother Lovie Nichols' name is brought up. She is a shining example of the power of persistence and perseverance. Her faith in Jesus Christ informs and directs everything she does whether it involves the leading of her family, ministry involvement and oversight and finally, the vehicle of prayer. The national prayer line that Mother Nichols started nearly two years ago has had an overarching impact across the country, encouraging believers and creating a new generation of Prayer Warriors. She has led by example, waking up every morning Monday-Friday at 5:00 a.m., faithfully. She not only organizes the call, but takes each and every prayer request, many times praying directly for the request in real-time. Many have commented that their lives have forever been changed as a result of participation.

Her central themes in prayer, tied to Luke 10:19, Hebrews 9:27 and Jeremiah 1:12 are expressed daily, and unapologetically. Beyond this gathering, Mother Nichols is one of the most down to earth, loving and caring people in the Body of Christ. She has taken on the role as spiritual mother for so many, pouring into their lives and providing reassurance based upon the Word of God. Her mantra is that "God's people need deliverance," and she is a conduit to that occurring because of her love for Christ and His people. The Kingdom of God is being advanced through her efforts.

Pastor Sandra Howell

Pastor Lovie Nichols, a woman of strength and integrity. Every area of her life exemplifies the depth to which she believes in the Word of God. Although an ordained pastor, she's known as "Mother Nichols" to most of her church family because she embodies the characteristics of a mother. She loves unequivocally, yet corrects swiftly. She embraced me and my daughters as her own, and I feel we are. I will always remember how she covered and nurtured me as a new member of our church, after spending most of my life in another church body. Mother

Nichols guided me through the new terrain, protecting me while I adapted to my new home. She consistently reminded me that I was where I belonged.

For that and numerous other reasons, I love you, Mother Nichols, and am forever indebted to you for your kindness. Continue to fulfill the promise of your mantra: "I hate the devil!"

Falana Johnson

Beautiful	Kind	Sweet	Gentle	Strong
Powerful	Loving	Unwavering	Anointed	Strict
Consistent	Wisdom	Encouraging	Firm	Unmovable
Unstoppable	Caring	Funny!!	Smart	Guidance
Helpful	Compassionate	Determined	Mindful	Servant
Counselor	Truthful	Mentor	Giving	Woman
Mother	Friend	Stern	Intercessor	Warrior!
Real!	Mighty	Source	Understanding	Patient

Above are a few of the descriptive words that Mother Lovie Nichols has been to my life. Beautiful, because you are so pretty. You have a heart of gold, and a smile that lights up the darkness in my day. I love to be in your presence.

I am so glad to have met you, Mother. I thank God for allowing me the opportunity to be in the presence of such wisdom, power and strength. I love the hate that you have for the devil. I pray for the same hate. Consistent because I have known her for years and her stance is still the same, except for being stronger with her hate for the devil and her love for God's people. Mother, you have helped me in so many ways. You encouraged me when I wanted to give up. You believed in me when I didn't believe in myself. You keep me going when I wanted to quit.

When things are not going as planned, the pressure is heavy and it's just hard, after one conversation with you I'm able to try again with a new plan. The pressure is lifted, and what was so hard now has a simple solution.

Thank you for never turning me away. When I come to you in a panic, you simply calm me down in your stern voice and say, "Awww that ain't nothing!" Do this, then that and WHAM the devil is defeated again. I fondly remember when my family was going through a hard time and you were right there praying, and helping us through. Mother, you were there for me through some really trying times, never turning me away. Always sharing wisdom and bringing me back to reality with the Word of God. I thank God for your voice, character and stance that are strictly sharp, like the double-edged sword.

Mother, you are beautiful inside and out. It is a pleasure to call you Mother. Thank you for every prayer. I can see the devil coming at me, but because of your prayers for me, he is stopped dead in his tracks. I Love You! I Love You! I Love You!

Evangelist Alma Lyons

One of the greatest privileges of my life is to be a Prayer Warrior along with Pastor Nichols. In the past eight years, I have witnessed the supernatural anointing of God in her life. Her surrendered life to God has manifested healing, deliverance and salvation for many souls. My family and I love her dearly, and call her "Mother." Mother has stood in the gap in prayer for sickness, and the attacks of the enemy in our lives. We love to hear her say, "I HATE THE DEVIL!"

This book is a must read for all ages. It is inspirational, challenging and sometimes funny. Her life story provides us with everyday challenges that we may all experience in our lives, but thank God that we, too, can be more than conquerors. I thank God for the life of this great woman of God, Pastor/Mother Lovie Nichols. May God continue to bless her life as she continues to walk with the Lord.

Evangelist Alma Lyons

Allen O'Banner

Godly Mother with Godly love, is treasure from God above. A Godly Mother with Godly care, has God's help when she says a prayer. Thank you, Momma, so very much for being my spiritual mom and for accepting me as your spiritual son. Momma, words cannot express the love that i have for you. Each time I'm on the phone with you, I feel like a little kid that can't wait to hear his mother's voice. Momma, you made me feel that I could talk to you about anything and everything. You encouraged me and let me know that I can do all things through Christ who strengthens me. Momma, you told me that whatever I'm going through, to let go and let God. Thank you, Momma Nichols, for being you! Much love for you always!

Elder Ozie Owen

Mother Nichols has been an incredible influence in helping me to understand true dependence upon the power of the Holy Spirit.

I will never forget how I was so busy in ministry, doing good works as the church newspaper editor, television ministry director, supporting fundraising on Saturdays, leading the aspiring minister's ministry, supporting the prison ministry, conducting public TV ministry meetings, plus I had a new wife and family with a full-time job in industry. At that time, the Lord was using Mother Nichols to conduct prayer and ministry on Sunday evenings at the church. Quite frankly, I was "afraid" of Mother Nichols. Her eyes pierced my very soul. I knew she was serious about God, and could see that I was caught up in activities as a "substitute" for intimacy with the Lord. I was convicted. One day, she approached me and told me that the Lord wanted me to pray. I will never forget what I was thinking during that time. I thought to myself, "I am too busy to spend time praying due to all my ministry obligations." But I knew she was right. One day, I attended her prayer service where she re-affirmed God's will for me to seek Him in prayer. She prayed for me and I reluctantly accepted.

Shortly after that, I went to Texas to do some ministry and I saw God move in ways I'd never witnessed before. I knew something was different, and I knew that the Lord had used Mother Nichols to show me His power. Within a few weeks, the Lord visited me in a way that radically changed my life, my walk, my prayer life, my ministry and my entire life. I had been baptized and filled with the Holy Ghost years before, but this was markedly different and revealing of the Person of God. During that time, Mother Nichols encouraged me and was always available to answer questions. She gave me worship tapes and some reading materials. She showed me love, kindness, acceptance and the Lord used her to help me in my spiritual journey.

Mother Nichols has the gift from the Lord to encourage and build up the wounded, the cast-down, rejected and hurting, that they might seek His face to fulfill God's plan for their lives. Her infectious enthusiasm for prayer and seeking God for instruction are an example for those she mentors, to be completely dependent on God for the very air they breathe.

I have personally witnessed Mother Nichols go through persecution and attacks by powerful ministries through the years. She endured with patience, love and refused to retaliate but would pray for those that accused her falsely. Her commitment to the Lord and steadfastness in "His Holiness" has been a part of her message, her conversation, her ministry and her life. Her humility and dependence upon the Holy Spirit underpins everything she does.

I have been both highly honored and blessed to be able to call her my sister, friend and mother in the Lord. She is truly one of God's mighty vessels in the Body of Christ, a warrior with an unconquerable commitment to serving our Lord and Savior Jesus, the Son of the Most High.

Minister Debra T. Pickett

I was first connected to Mother Lovie Nichols through a fast sisterhood friendship with the late Minister Gloria Crawford from New Life Covenant Church Southeast. Through Gloria's introduction to Mother Nichols, I was drafted to the early morning prayer line and quickly came to know and understand that Mother Nichols possessed great inner-strength, a profound faith in God and an intolerance for satan's presence anywhere, except under her feet! We were alike in all of those ways. She overtly expresses that she "hates the devil," and I proclaim that I have a love/hate relationship with him: I love to hate him. More personally, I discovered that Mother Nichols and I are both camera shy, but will submit to the lens only under necessary circumstances. I love her dearly.

In April of 2016, I was devastated after losing the two women in ministry with whom I had first became connected after joining New Life Covenant, within three days of each other. The Lord sent Mother Lovie Nichols, being only herself, to fill both empty spaces in my life with her love, strength and spiritual wisdom. It is an honor to be connected with her in spirit and in truth! And, what should be said about one woman's life of prayer that has ignited and intensified the prayer lives of so many others? Not a little! Her life is a living example and often reminds all of us of something my Aunt Katherine Bynum would always say: Much prayer, Much Power; Little Prayer, Little Power; No Prayer, No Power! Mother Lovie Nichols possesses MUCH POWER!

To me, she is:

> A gifted mentor, the answer to a prayer
> An anchor of hope, when I experienced despair.
> A source of strength, in the midst of pain.
> A source of heaven's light, in the midst of life's rain.
> She seeks neither this world's fortune, nor fame;
> But, who she is and all she does, is done in Jesus' name.

Minister Carolyn Powell

Words can never express the many attributes this wonderful woman of God exhibits. I first met Pastor Nichols in the mid 1980's, and we have been friends ever since. She had a strong faith in God and her personality displayed this relationship. Pastor Lovie Nichols loves young people, she loves the house of God and she also loves her leaders. The number one outstanding quality is her strong prayer life. She fits all of the qualifications of a true warrior for God. She is a woman of authority, and her heavenly language flows in a powerful way.

Pastor Nichols has a great testimony and teaches her children how to pray. She prays for all of her children, and continues to do so even now. I remember when I was invited to be the guest speaker at Center of Hope. I will never forget it because it was my first speaking engagement. The Lord gave me a word of prophecy that this woman would be a pastor. She was not pastoring then, but she is now! God's word is true! I saw it come to pass with my own eyes!

I know that this book will encourage many to write their stories, and I know it will bring deliverance to many. Thank God for this great woman of God. I also want to thank God for the power of deliverance that flows in her life. She has a heart to see God's people delivered. Pastor Nichols would oftentimes tell us about how God said, "My people need to be delivered." It was because of this need, that the Lord gave her a vision to start a daily prayer line where hundreds of people are trained as intercessors and Prayer Warriors.

I thank God for this great woman of God, who has consistently obeyed the call to pray and raise up intercessors, and pray for our pastors and leaders and church mothers. I have heard great testimonies of how God miraculously worked miracles. The things that man said was impossible, God made possible through the power of prayer. I truly believe that at this stage in this great woman of God's life, she is not intimidated by others, and is on an assignment for God. She loves to see the power of God demonstrated in His people. I thank God for Pastor Lovie Nichols.

Joi Thomas

Pastor Nichols is a faith believing, devil-chasing, powerful woman of God. Also, she's an answer to my prayers. These days, very few people take the time out for single/divorced mothers.

I'd desired someone to look beyond my past/present and see what I saw: "The greatness of God" in the foundation of my life. God called Pastor Lovie Nichols. Her first name alone was signature enough. "Lovie," because love is what I needed. I needed someone to teach me how to love.

Pastor Nichols is an example of the masterpiece God had in mind when He said, "Let the elder women teach the younger women." From the first day I met her, she prayed for me and then pointed me toward my destiny! Many people say they have been blessed from the ministry of worship I do at NLC-SE. But many don't know that it was/is Pastor Nichols who encourages me to be the worshiper that God wants me to be! Broken as a pastor's daughter, God used Pastor Nichols through prayer, counseling, mentorship and faith in His timing. I am no longer in pieces, but am a vessel of worship, prayer, love and joy. Pastor Nichols is dear and special to me; her kindness has been as a friend, prayer partner, counselor, mentor and she is a great instrument of the circle that God uses to orchestrate His purpose through my life. She has stood in faith with me through homelessness, and many other challenges, and now because of her faith I am employed with the State of Illinois, providing for my own family, and driving my own car.

Diane Thompson

I met Pastor Nichols eight years ago, through Robyn Williams. Pastor Nichols and I have remained very close friends. She reminds me so much of my grandmother. She's been my mentor, my strength and my angel. I can call her anytime and she has always been there to listen. One thing I know about Pastor Nichols is that she "hates the devil." She is a true Christian and she loves God. I love Pastor Nichols, because she is honest and she will always tell you what the Word of God says. Thank you, Pastor Nichols, for being my friend. I love you.

Pastor Doris Thompson

I am so blessed to have a friend and co-worker like Pastor Lovie Nichols. She has truly been a blessing to me. When we first met at New Life Covenant Church, hosted at King High School, I knew immediately that she was a woman of God. She was like a quiet storm. She always prayed throughout the service. I know for a fact that she kept Pastor Hannah and his wife, Anna Hannah, covered in prayer.

We became closer when we decided to go to a Benny Hinn conference in Indianapolis, Indiana. We shared about our families and struggles throughout our lives. Pastor Nichols shared anecdotes about her children, and I shared about mine. One of the most significant things she shared was how much she loved to see souls saved. That was so important in her life. As the Lord began to bless and save souls at New Life, she stated, "I don't have to go to the Benny Hinn conference anymore, because souls are being save at New Life."

When the Lord assigned her to start the 5:30 a.m. prayer line, I was reluctant to yield to the call to wake up that early in the morning. When I finally decided to join the prayer line, it was truly a blessing. I can say the daily commitment to pray for the needs of others has been a blessing to me. Pastor Nichols loves to help the people of God, and to encourage others. I have truly been encouraged by her ministry of prayer and intercession.

Amanda Treadwell

Mother Pastor Nichols has been a blessing in my life since the day she entered it. I thank God that she took me under her wing and helped me in an area in which I felt that I was weak.

She encouraged me to be better, and follow God in all His ways. I'm truly thankful. Thank you! I just personally want to thank you for reaching out to me on Facebook. You just don't know that praying has been one of my weaknesses. Growing up, I felt I didn't know how to pray. But now, I have that urge to want to become better to allow God to use me and my words to help others. I thank God for you every day because you didn't have to do that for me. And, I'm so happy you grabbed a hold of me and took me under your wing. I love you, Mother. You are changing my life for the better. Forever, you are my spiritual grandmother.

Rosie Warren-Hall

Mother Nichols, I thank God for you being in my life! God put you in my life for a reason, and not for a season. He knew my journey so he put you in my life. You are someone I look up to. You are a generous and caring person. You are a true friend who really cares. You are my superhero. I can call you at any time of the day, or night and you have a listening ear. You are a person that I admire, and have the utmost love and respect for. You are someone I simply think the world of. My goodness, but I love you so much...now and forever more!

Minister C. Terrell Wheat

If I could use but one word to describe what Pastor Nichols has been to me, that word would be lifesaver. I would not be who I am without Pastor Nichols. There are only a handful of people that I trust with my most pressing prayer needs, and Pastor Nichols is one of those people. Pastor Nichols has always been there for me. She has been an encourager in my darkest hours. She has been an advisor when I've faced tough decisions. She has been my counselor when I've gotten off track. But most of all, she has prayed for me. Pastor Nichols is an intercessor for intercessors! I never would have made it without Pastor Nichols, and I thank God for her daily.

Minister Charlom Wilcher

You love God, and He knows you love Him. Stay with Him and He will make you a pillar for His Glory." Those were the words shared with me by (at the time) Mother Lovie Nichols on the altar, after prayer some 10 years ago. Pastor Nichols has proven to be a woman of great faith in our Lord and Savior Jesus Christ. It is that faith which drives her motivation to encourage us younger women to "Walk with God," as she so often admonishes.

Pastor is a staple for us here at New Life. Her stance in God gives us all a glimpse of His miraculous power bestowed upon humanity. Her overcoming rejection within the Body of Christ, battling an ailment with skin disease and taking care of her loving husband, whom she knew would eventually forget many things, has been one of the greatest examples of being steadfast, immovable and always abounding in the work of the Lord. We all owe God a great deal of gratitude for giving us a believer who loves Him so much that she'd make the sacrifice of living her life in way that encourages us all to do the same, walk with God.

Pastor Nichols is a life-saver for many of us through her prayers and words of wisdom. We are eternally grateful for her life story and its impact upon each of us. Thank you, Lord, for Pastor Lovie Nichols: A woman, a wife, a mother, a leader, a Pastor and servant. She's one of the greatest ministry gifts ever given to the Body of Christ. We pray that her story blesses and touches your life, as deeply as it has our own. We love you, Pastor Nichols!

Pamela Williams

I was going through a rough time in my life. One day, I was talking to my sister-in-law about the challenge I was dealing with daily. I had been going through this for eight years. My sister-in-law told me about the prayer line that Mom Nichols hosts daily at 5:30 a.m. She encouraged me to listen to it. She said it would really bless my life.

About two months ago, I started listening and asking for prayer for myself and my family. When I first started listening, I told her I was new to the prayer line. She welcomed me, and prayed for my situation at that time. About two days went by, when I received a call from her. She prayed for me and my issues. She has been helping me ever since. I had the pleasure of meeting her in person and also introduced her to my husband and daughter. She is truly a strong woman of God. Her spirit and her strength continuously encourages me daily. She is a wonderful person. She talks to me as if I am her child, and I love that about her.

I can talk to her about anything. She always gives me the best advice on how to handle a situation and it all reflects back to the Bible. She always lets me know that whatever I'm going through, it's in the Bible, and God can direct me on what to do. She's there whenever I need her. She is a person that when I'm feeling down, her spirit lifts me up. Her words touch my heart, and she reminds me never to give up on God and to stay in my Word because God will perfect those things that concern me. Mom Nichols lets me know that God will deliver my child, and for me not to worry because doing so is not of God.

Being around her and talking to her has truly uplifted my spirits, and helped me to not be afraid of anything. I've learned to take all of my cares to God, because He will work it out for me. Without her helping me, listening to me and encouraging me, I would still be feeling sad and defeated. So, I thank God that He brought her into my life...at just the right time.

• • • •